MW00975682

It Wasn't You, It Was Me

María de la Luz Gutiérrez

Author María de la Luz Gutiérrez

Maria de la Luz Gutiérrez
ISBN: 978-1-7368650-2-6
Made in U.S.A
Book cover Valerie I Suárez
visuarez02@gmail.com

GRATITUDE

I thank my Almighty Father God, for his support in this difficult process in my life, I know that He always supported me, that I was never alone.

To the angels of heaven who took care of me in the most dangerous moments and watched over my dream.

To my mother who was my guide with her truth, love, and affection, supporting me to get ahead.

To my children for all the love, support, and patience, especially Valerie who was always like an eagle, watching out for me.

To my son Miguel who always trusted me, and I felt his unconditional love.

To my Abigail, who amazes me with her individuality, independence, love of life, and she let me be.

To my high school friends Martha, Estela, and Carmen for their unconditional support, especially Estela for her patience and understanding.

To Kobe Bryant for his hard work that inspired me.

DEDICATION

This book is dedicated to my dad who is in heaven. I thank you for being my father. I know that, although he is already on another astral plane, he is still watching me, as he always will.

I am grateful to God that he gave me the opportunity to say goodbye to him. I had a family wedding engagement that prevented me from going to visit him in those days, but something told me that I needed to be with him, so I suspended the engagement and went with him.

¡It was the last time I was going to see him! All the time I felt a strange sensation, which made me remember every moment that I lived with him.

I could tell you many things about my father, but I like to remember the moments that I enjoyed with him, so I am going to tell you a funny anecdote:

I wanted to go to the Villa, where the Basilica of Guadalupe is, to see my friend Maru and my dad told me not to go. I said to him: "Apa, but how can I not go? And he replied:" You are not here in the United States! And the only way you're going is for me to take you. "

He made me laugh a lot, and I told him that I was no longer a little girl, but at the same time I knew that for him I was still his little girl and he wanted to protect me, so if that gave him peace, why not let him take me. So we went in the taxi.

On the way it occurred to me to take a photo of us, and I laughed a lot in that moment, when we took the last selfie, in the Villa we got out of the taxi, we walked for a while and I touched his hand. I could feel and see his worn skin, I took him by his arm, and we continued walking.

I think on that occasion he was saying goodbye to me, because he gave me several errands I told him: ¡ Apa, we still need to go to Cuba! He looked at me and said no! ...! No longer! At that moment I didn't understand it, but now I know.

When I was coming back to the U.S. He did not sleep, he was careful not to be late, because I was going to fly at dawn. We were two hours before the indicated time at the airport. When we said goodbye at the entrance, I took his hand, gave him a soft kiss on the cheek, said goodbye to him, and I thought: "I want to remember this moment as if it were the last time", and it was.

He knew I was writing this book and he told me, "*Maria, but when are you going to finish it?*" I told him soon, I hope very soon, but I had many setbacks.

Next time I called to Mexico, I didn't want him to ask me, I just wanted to surprise him that the book was already finished, but I was surprised, because I thought I had all the time in the world and no! We went through the pandemic and my dad went to heaven.

Now that I've finished it, I dedicate all the effort and my triumph to him. I know that I have his blessing and love from heaven.

When I realized that God had given me the opportunity to say goodbye to my dad, I was happy with his departure.

If you are reading, and you could not say goodbye to a loved one and their departure still hurts, I want to tell you that heaven and earth are one, there are no limits or borders. It may be that you can't see it, but you can feel it, so be positive and express love to feel comfortable letting go. Then you will be able to speak with your loved ones who are present from another dimension, because they can hear you. Say goodbye to them with love and allow them to leave in peace.

"Apá, I know that you are listening to me from heaven, and I send you a hug and a kiss with all my love to where you are, and I tell you that I love you. I know that I am your female version, because we are so alike in so many way.

I love you Apa, see you later."

INTRODUCTION

It Wasn't You, It Was Me

This is a book made for those of us who suffered a love breakup, a divorce… ¡An emotional loss! Many of us have been through this process at some point.

When we go out looking for love, we have extremely high expectations, and we are looking for the ideal prospect that fits our personality and has similar tastes to ours. When it is the time of the courtship everything is understanding and sweet, it is the stage of infatuation that can last up to three years, when that energy passes, that love is transformed into something more solid and becomes more penetrating; the person shows themself as they are, without masks to please.

For those who only wanted to enjoy that stage of falling in love, it's not so painful, because when this stage is over, they simply withdraw and leave. This is where the pain begins for the person who loved the most, surrendered and lost the most, because they made high expectations that seemed valid to them, reflecting the relationship at the beginning.

In addition to my experience, I learned in a field study I did, the breakup hurts the same at any age, whether you're 13 years old or 80 years old, it hurts the same. It doesn't matter if you are a girlfriend, boyfriend, husband, wife or none. Love is love, and it has your essence and intensity.

When you are in deep pain, you get carried away by emotions and sink into a chaos of ideas, thoughts and feelings that overwhelm you, sinking into a depression that paralyzes your life, from which it can take years to recover and, in some cases, a lifetime.

This made me reflect and write about the emotional process of my divorce. I spent a long time immersed in pain, the more I thought, the more I sank into the mud of depression: when you are in that emotional state, you don't pay attention to your logic, or profession ... you just want to live in pain; the body gets used to everything, you become addicted to the emotion of pain and you adapt to being "the one who suffered."

I realized that I was in this situation and took therapy, in addition to the hypnotherapy healing practices, that I practice to this day, and it freed me faster than I expected.

I was working emotion by emotion and not release it until I was healed and then released. I did my field work and realized how many people are trapped in a similar or the same emotional situation and need this information.

In my case, I went through this alone, I felt like I was trapped in a maze of terrible emotions and I wanted someone to help me, but I felt that they did not understand my pain, so I closed myself off.

If you are going through a situation like this, I want to tell you that I do understand your pain, that you are not alone, and that you are going to come out of this crisis with triumph.

YOU LEFT STEALTHILY

I didn't say goodbye to you!
If I had known I was going to lose you...
I would have made it....

From that man who made me very happy and who fell in love with me,
I would have thanked him

because he taught me to live a romance that I never imagined, he filled my life with details, attentions, caresses
that made me reach the sky.

The love taught me to
caress the clouds
flying with the wind,
to dance in the rain,
to feel the sun's rays caress my hair.
He made me feel like the most beautiful woman, like a rare jewel,
I felt like the flowers, full of color,
his voice whispered beautiful words that made me enter a world full of love that was only for me.
His sweetness and tenderness made fille me with joy, I felt special valued and protected, because he gave me the best of him.

Love is beautiful, but you have to know how to live and accept it when it ends, because, just as it appears, one day it also disappears.

Who captivated your gaze?
Where are you?
¡It makes me jealous to know that I don't have you anymore!... that you left and took a part of me with you... I can't find myself and I'm wandering adrift... I've already lost you!

I'm lonely, my love cries, cries without you...
Why did you leave me? what will become of me without you?

I FOUND MYSELF

My soul walks without you...
it looks for you with its eyes,
but you are no longer with me, my soul.
I see your face.
and I look in your eyes for something of me,
but nothing remains... nothing from me.

My sad soul realizes that I've already lost you.
I lost you forever,
what will become of me?
Night comes... dark nights...
cold and long, long and cold without you.
I shelter alone, you're not here anymore!

I reach out my arm,
I search for your shoulder,
my hand is lost, I never find you,
I wrap myself in my grief,
I find no comfort.

I cry at night,
and I tell my soul to settle.

that I've already lost you and you're not coming.
Days and nights go by and by,
the loneliness overwhelms me,
the cold envelops me.

My soul looks at me with tenderness.
and gives me comfort,
warms me with its breath...
fills and shelters me.

I feel relief...
the pain is diminishing,
I sigh, I breathe, I inhale deeply, and I smile.
I find myself,
I am recognizing myself,
I talk to myself and listen to me singing.

I walk lightly and smiling,
I go admiring the flirtatious flowers that dance and sing for me,
I feel happy, the pain is passing, I can feel it.
I am content, life is coming back,
I'm happy, happy to have me and to feel me,
I came back home; I came back to me...
I felt, I lived, and I was thankful...
everything happens for a reason,
and God wanted it that way.

SOUL SEDUCTION

When we meet our partner,
we know it is the ideal one, we are impressed from the first moment we see them. Then something in us is transformed, and their being attracts us like a magnet. The world around us seems wonderful and a joy that we have never felt before awakens.

We are happy to think that we share the same world with its air, a sun that shines on us and gives us warmth, and a moon that, although we are separated, he sees at night and knows that it is the same one that sees us both and shelters us with its rays of light.

! Love is marvelous!
If love is so wonderful, ¿why does it end?
¿What happens?
¿Why does one of the two lose more than the other?
or
¿Why suffer more when the relationship breaks up?
The most important factor is attachment.
The person who suffers the most from loss is the one whose soul was seduced, whose heart was touched, who was captivated to the point of losing themself in the essence of the other.

HIS PERSONALITY DROVE YOU CRAZY

Everyone has a way of doing things, there are strategies even to seduce someone "fall in love" and that is what gives personality and individuality to each human being, creating a unique spark of energy that sweeps. That makes people fall in love creating bonds of attraction, empathy, charisma, seduction, and sexuality.

"The essence" of the person is what you desire most. You go crazy thinking about their self, their body scent, their voice, the way they walk, their attitude towards the world around them, along with the way they treat you and see things, all this creates a physical, mental, and chemical attraction.

The emotion is triggered when you see or think about that person, and that is what drives you crazy and you lose your willpower.

THE WOMAN SURRENDERS BY EAR

The man sweetens the woman's ear with words that she wants to hear. He knows the truth about her, and with that he knows that he will win her over, he creates a fantasy that for her is a reality, "he seduces her soul."

The man knows how to lower the sky and sweeten the palate, even if what the woman hears are lies. She enjoys it to the fullest and he creates a perfect world with her truths, not from him.

No matter how old you are, you can sweeten the ear of anyone who wants to listen and enjoy.

After self-deception, recognizing the truth hurts, even if it sets you free, dig into the truth, even if it is painful, to destroy the lie and the obsession.

When you love yourself, you will have the realization and the strength to not allow petty words to take away your will, because after a good verb, you will have to give something,

Remember that desire is disguised as romantic dreams, they begin with words that create emotions that alter your senses, that produces pure adrenaline, you feel alive, but just as easy as they give them to you, the day you least expect it, they will also snatch it away from you just like that. They sweeten your ear and then they go away.

LOVE IN MY WAY

I wanted love to be my way, just as we all long to be loved and reciprocated with the same intensity, to be like a fairy tale and to last forever.

You play with illusion and create your own world full of fantasy, you idealize how you would like to be loved and you take for granted that he understands your love, that he loves you in the same way.

For me, he was part of me, I felt a spiritual connection, I thought we had the same beliefs and convictions, I felt we formed a unique couple.

We talked about our expectations, with a marriage full of love and trust. I also remember that on several occasions we talked about how our life together was going to be, and we told each other that our marriage did not have to end like most of the couples we knew, that as time goes by, they become boring.

We created rules based on the mistakes we saw in other couples, and analyzing, we deduced where they failed, we thought that with our love we were sure it was going to be different, we loved each other, and we wanted a marriage for life.

But that changed due to lack of commitment, responsibility, and emotional stability. It's very easy to talk, but keeping a commitment to someone is difficult, and it's easier to become forgetful.

You take it for granted that the person will deliver what they promised.

BELIEFS AND CONVICTIONS IN MARRIAGE

Love is idealized, and I do believe it!
My convictions to marriage were commitment, fidelity, loyalty, empathy, reciprocity to the relationship, and I always kept it until the end.

My beliefs, values and convictions come from my roots, that is what lead me to respect such an important commitment as marriage.

This illusion comes from my childhood and I idealized it.

When it was my wedding, I had a wonderful experience, with my beautiful white dress, I felt like a princess.

No one had ever done anything special for me. But that day, the love, and attention as for me, I felt loved, protected, and admired, I felt fulfilled.

HOW A WOMAN PROJECTS HERSELF

I was apparently calm, I dedicated myself to the care and education of my children and household activities. My youngest son consumed most of my time with special chores and sports, which required a lot of dedication and effort,
I still made time to read and write about topics that were important to me.

On one occasion, I went to a workshop that dealt with "How to improve as a couple." At the end of the workshop, the lecturer and I talked for a long time and then she asked me a question, ***"how I felt about my relationship with my partner."*** I answered with "fine," then I continued commenting on how my relationship was, to which she told me: *"that is what you have created, peace, harmony and an apparent happiness, but that is nothing more yours, it is what you are, what you project, and what you give. That is, you, not your partner."*
Each person projects their reality, their being, and what they want to create for others.

After meditating and observing my beliefs and thoughts, I realized my original projections and that was to be faithful and devoted to my marriage, too bad his reality was different.

EVERYTHING CHANGES, EVEN LOVE

Everything changes, everything transforms, even love. Love can grow or end. What one day you like and drives you crazy, stops moving your floor, and over the years it can end. It is difficult to accept that they no longer want to love you, what one day was a lifeline in happiness, became a labyrinth.

Change is imminent and I had to accept that the person I loved was gone, his illusion, his passion. He was no longer mine and I had to let him go. It hurts, it hurts a lot, it is a slap to the ego, and it is said that if you love something, let it go, and I said, "but he is already gone!"

To let go of the hooks that have trapped your soul, to understand that even without you, he could make a life and be happy, it hurts, and it hurts a lot, but in the end, you let go and when you let go it hurts even more, you feel that the soul is torn and now you must have to heal from each tear. You return to your place of departure healthy and clean.

Now I focus on me! Loss is just a matter of focus.

WOMEN'S TANTRUMS

I look for your attention
and I do everything to make you look at me,
I get carried away like the chilindrina
crying and being dramatic.

I want to have my partner's attention
and I do everything I can to make you look at me,
and I look like a child with no control
due to impotence and frustration.

I blurt out all the accusations to make you feel bad,
but really,
all I want is for you to tell me that you were wrong,
that you want my love,
and that you are going to do everything you can
to make us right.

¡How hard it is to think about before
and after!
Reality makes you wake up
and see that you are stuck
in emotions of frustration,
because of the pain of having lost
your love; I have so much courage!
¡I want to get even!
¡I want to make you suffer!
It is useless to invest more time

and feel more pain.
It is hooking me more to you,
although I feel impotence and frustration,
I have to let you go
clean without you taking anything from me,
I have given you enough.

¡Go away and don't come back!
I don't want you here anymore!
Take the last of your things
with you because afterwards,
I don't know how I'll react without you...

DOMINATES AS IF HE WERE ITS MASTER

Who loves more, loses more. In a relationship there is someone who imposes more on the other. The weaker one, afraid of losing the relationship, leaves his /her personal preferences to please the other and adopt the personality of the partner.

They become so interpenetrated that they lose their personality and individuality, and when the relationship ends, she does not find herself, she does not know what to do with herself, because by copying the other, she has become empty.

FEAR PARALYZED ME

I was afraid, afraid of losing the person with whom I shared more than half of my life.

He was part of me, I felt that part of my soul was being torn away. His departure was imminent, I felt that he was like sand in my hands that was slipping through my fingers, and I asked myself ¿why so much struggle? ¿why so much fear and pain?

The struggle was with myself: He didn't even realize all my emotional battles, and if he even noticed, he didn't care. It was a struggle, but... I didn't know who I was fighting against.

When it was all over, I could see it, I could feel it. I was paralyzed by fear, but I still fought, and when I felt it intensely, I held firm not to lose control of myself.

I was experiencing a grief, a loss, I felt depressed, and I asked myself, ¿why? and I found the answer: You lose part of you when that person leaves.

When a partner joins you, you form a single energetic structure that is part of your essence, energy, smell and aura and you integrate with that person becoming one. When the relationship breaks up, there is no longer an exchange of nurturing energy, and the person automatically feels depressed, desolate, sad, and withered. They go into emotional shock and fear the loss.

SMOKE VEIL TO AVOID SEEING THE REALITY

You do not want to see the signs of deception, of "infidelity", because if you accept them, you have to face fears and emotions that destabilize your interior, you face the doubt of whether he still loves you.

Between fear, uncertainty, your ability to survive alone, so many responsibilities, still young children who do not want marriage and home to break up, there comes a time when you get under a veil of smoke, to see neither accept reality.

There is naivety in many people who cannot imagine the behavior of an unfaithful person, the ability to lie and act normal in front of their partner, who never doubts her.

Innocent people do not see these signs because they do not know them, what the husband

does may seem strange to him, but he does not care because he does not know what is behind each action, because the brain has not registered it, it registers it as a simple fact, until you have knowledge of the action, the information arrives and the changes begin,
listen, look" someone comments on it. It is until that moment that he begins to suspect.

It is difficult for innocent minds to see signs of infidelity, when there is no deception in their spirit, they can be very wise in other areas of their lives, but not in the vile and lies.

I reproached myself many times, ¡how I had been so deluded! ¡Why hadn't he done anything before! ¡ Why the deception! And I read a phrase that said: "Blessed are the innocent, they do not suffer because they do not see the wickedness of the wicked."

When you have an innocent mind, you always have confidence in people, you cannot imagine the nefarious actions that they can carry out, such as infidelity or cheating.

?WHAT AM I GOING TO DO WITH ME?

¡I feel so lonely!

¡I am nowhere to be found!
they changed my settings.

What I recognized as mine
and made me feel happy,
I no longer have it.
I feel lost... I am afraid
and now ?what am I going to do with myself...?

The way in which I knew how to exist
has changed ...and I find myself
trying to recognize myself
and put together what is left of me.

¡I have to change,
and I am very afraid...
¡I don't know where to start
or what to do,
the world in which I felt so safe
and "protected"
where I knew how to manage myself,
has vanished.

I have to learn to restructure myself,
recognize who I am

and create a new "me"
so that I can subsist emotionally
living here and now.

I FOUND ANGELS ALONG THE WAY

In different instances of my life, I found wise people who gave me their love, support and understanding unconditionally. People who did not even know me, my history, my ups and downs but who gave me their advice with such value that they transformed my day and my life with innovative ideas, leading me on the path of truth, of my truth.

Therefore, I felt confidence in my decisions with immense satisfaction, despite the hardest process of my life, I found that angelic support.

I DIDN'T WANT YOU TO BE WRONG

By accepting that you were no longer interested in my feelings, or my pain, that ¡woke me up!

The love I had for him one day, made me feel hope to keep trying to rescue the relationship and him too, because I thought I was wrong.

I wanted him to see and value the life we had formed together and that we were a beautiful family, that we were a couple like few others because we radiated love. I tried to persuade him to make things right, but nothing worked. His disinterested attitude surprised me.

Possibly there were many warning signs that I didn't see, or if I noticed them, I didn't give them the real importance, because it was as if I had suddenly discovered him like that.

I trusted that the love that I contributed for both of us was enough, I believed in a unique, true and unbreakable love, but I had not realized that the love that he contributed, long ago no longer existed, I understood that to love you need two.

I said goodbye to the beautiful love that I gave and that he did not know how to appreciate. In the future, I know that someone will come along who will know how to value, appreciate and feel it, but above all that it will be reciprocal, because in the end that giving remains in me to be shared

I SAW YOU AND I DIDN'T KNOW YOU

I had the idea that you would come to your senses,
that you would make up for my suffering,
that we would be happy again,
that was my illusion,
but you changed so much
that the person I saw in front of me
was a total and perfect stranger
to my soul, my mind and my heart;
you were no longer the person I loved one day,
and neither was your soul,
¿why did you change so much?
it was as if you had been replaced
by another person who was alien to you.

WHEN RESPECT GETS LOST, EVERYTHING GETS LOST

You moved away from me
to have the freedom
to fill yourself with forbidden pleasures,
and you did not realize
how far you were corrupted,
you moved so far away that I could no longer save you,
you looked at me differently,

you became arrogant, despot and rude.

You put yourself on such a high pedestal
that you felt unreachable
and I did not deserve you...
you liked to be admired
and you became more demanding than ever,
you told me "you do not take care of me as I deserve"
and worst of all, ¡I believed it!

I was trying harder and harder ...
and it was never enough for you,
everything was missing or had something left over,
¡you were unbearable!

When we went out,
your gaze was always on someone,
which of course wasn't me,
you wanted me to praise you,
¡to take care of you like a god!
Reality came to me all at once,
your life seemed so fake,
you felt you deserved everything
and now you wanted me to pay your price.
I was no longer willing to tolerate it.
Your fantasy you had created
based on paid attentions
that made you feel like a king,

your demand for attention was illogical,
and for the first time
I realized that you were a narcissist and manipulator,
while at the same time,
ironically,
you were manipulated
by other people's conveniences.

Your ego and fantasies
made you lose reality.
Admiration and pleasure
became an addiction for you.

In truth, I loved,
admired and respected you,
but when trust was broken,
all that vanished,
and everything was lost in the relationship.

AT LAST, THE REALITY

You idealize and create a prince when he's a toad.

Seeing his inclination and attention with the person who maintained a relationship for such a long time. The time he devoted to each call in the morning, afternoon or evening. The affection and love with which he spoke to her and everything he said to her, it was a very strong emotional connection (don't ask me how, but I knew it, I knew it and that was enough) my beliefs, emotions and projects went to hell and the pedestal where I had him fell, crashed, shattered, there was no point in wanting to repair it. This brought me down, at least, the uncertainty was over, but what was happening at that moment... I never imagined it coming!

¡I'm not crazy, no! ¡I'm not crazy! it was a reality, far or not it's already ¡thundered!

LOVE GOES AWAY AND EVERYTHING LOOKS STRANGE

The more you love your partner, and he/she stops loving you, the more the world falls apart, you see everything strangely. The environment changes, the energy that filled you as a partner you no longer receive it, you begin to stop feeling the emotional, spiritual, and physical connection, everything is a void.

Everything that was familiar to your eyes no longer exists, your reality is no longer the same, your soul feels the loneliness, the abandonment and it hurts to the bone. The abstinence syndrome begins. Little by little, this begins to pass when you change your reality and focus on modifying your routine. The movement of doing new things changes your energy.

For example, walks on the beach, in the mountains, in the woods, gardening, you begin a connection with nature. The earth nurtures you and you create a bond of love and harmony with mother earth.

LIVING IN TWO REALITIES

To live in two worlds at the same time: one real and cruel, the other emotional and rapturous. That is why it is very difficult to get out of a relationship that produces so many mixed feelings and emotions that confuse us and provoke an internal struggle.

This is logical, we are emotional and rational beings, each experience has an emotion with its own chemistry in the body and is created with the secretion of hormones that are activated according to the situation.

The memory of situations lived in certain experiences of life, such as smells, flavors, colors, a song, a movie, a place, and even the environment, is imprinted, although we do not realize it, in the body memory.

We feel all these emotions when we bring them back to our memory, because the brain captures what we do not perceive with our eyes. Everything is in our subconscious and is activated by external reality.

They are reactions of the human being, which is what gives flavor to life, otherwise we would be pure zombies.

THE BRAIN WORKS AGAINST YOU

Feelings sweep everything away and it seems that when you most want to forget, the brain does the opposite, it brings back more memories and plays against you, you want to stop eating and you get hungrier, you want to forget and the memory appears out of nowhere, a photo, the dress you wore at a party, an anniversary, etc.

The decision is more effective when you can have emotional control.

EMOTION TORTURES YOU

The only way to control the thought is to manage the emotion. When I felt that the emotion was dominating me, I did not resist, I let it come, I annulled the feeling, I did not pay attention to it or to my time, until it faded away by itself away by itself, it is easier said than done, but after losing so much, you do not want or have to continue losing more, and even if you don´t have the will , you must do it, you must not stay stuck in something that has no sense and that only cause you pain and sorrow.

UNDERSTANDING MY EMOTIONS SO THAT THEY NO LONGER TORMENT ME

¡I recognized myself! ¡ I knew who I am¡, ¡what I am like! what is mine and what I want for myself and for my life. To reach this stage of recognition, I had to project myself from the inside out. Outside the situation that tormented me and the emotions that kept me in a whirlpool full of confusion and mental chaos, generating mixed feelings.

The memories were tormenting me, I didn't know how to stop them. When you are like this, you don't have your feet on the ground, it is as if you are deprogrammed of who you are and the emotional being that we all carry inside comes out and the emotions sweep you away.

If you are going through a situation of heartbreak and loss and you can't deal with it, it is best to seek professional help to guide you in deciphering your emotions.
It is important to trust someone to guide or accompany you through this experience, which can last a long time, before you become stuck and frustrated.

Find a person with whom you can talk and feel comfortable, it can be a sibling, a friend, either close or at a distance; but very important, it has to be someone who will not judge you no matter what you say and who will be there for you, at the moment you need him or her the most.

I mention this because I wanted to do it alone and I was lost and frustrated for a long time. When I got the support of a very dear unconditional friend, she helped me to understand and get out of the emotions that kept me going round and round, leaving me exhausted, without resolving anything.

IT'S NOT LOVE, IT'S OBSESSION

You beg as if he would pity you, he does not love you.

He does not even love himself: he does not know what love is. The unfaithful person plays with love, plays with the feelings of the one who gives him his attention, thinks only of his desires, what fills him and makes him go out of reality. They are characteristics of an unfaithful person.
Giver of nothing, demanding everything.
An unconscious where the woman is a game and is an object in his hands.
He will bend the woman with sweetness to fill himself with her, when a novelty appears that fills his taste, they leave without any type of remorse.
His motto: talk to the woman about love and sincerity until she believes it.

A NARCISIST

He was always looking after me, he would open the car door, he would put me in the chair, he was very thoughtful, he would give me a ring for every anniversary. We liked to go to places and have a drink, it was a very nice relationship. We would go out with friends (other couples) and he was always looking out for me.

The couples we went out with were very surprised, *especially the women who were in a bad marriage.* If I forgot something in the car, he would offer to bring it. For me those details were normal, and they were amazed because there was a lot of understanding and empathy between us, even after so many years of marriage, and I could feel it, and of course, I was happy.

But this gradually changed, he liked very much the admiration he caused in women. He was attentive to them, attentive to bring them a drink or to pay attention to them, and they always sat in front of us to get his attention.

I told him to keep his distance from them, the situation was annoying and uncomfortable, and they could misinterpret him. He kept his distance, but there was always someone who approached, not that he was so handsome, but when a woman sees another woman who has the attention and special treatment of a man, it makes them envious: because he has what they crave in a relationship, and they approach him like flies to honey.

I could see how his vanity grew, he liked the flattery, and his airs and graces began to rise. Yes, I noticed it...but we were having a great time with a group of friends, and I didn't think much of it until his attitude changed drastically.

At that time, he changed jobs and started working where he always wanted to work, and that's when his change was radical. He would arrive later than usual, he would suddenly leave the house, I would tell him "I'm coming with you" and he would say no...

He always had a considerable amount of money in his wallet, but from one day to the next ¡he no longer had any! I would ask him "¿what did you do with the money?" and he would answer me rambling "I used it for this or that." Then he would say flatly "it's my money" ¡no!

He covered the expenses and needs of the house and I didn't need anything, in the end he would say "¡you already have your money, let me spend mine!"

I didn't see where he spent the money and his attitude towards me was no longer the same. When we went out, he really liked the attention of mutual friends, they behaved more daring and flirtatious and were not interested if their attitude bothers me at all that, at this point, he was already very distant from me he behaved very arrogant, he made me feel like I didn't deserve him, his vanity grew to the sky.

He had created a prestige for himself, the cool one, the one who pays for everything. Their admiration became his pleasure.
I knew deep inside that the relationship was bad, but I had emotions like a roller coaster: some days I was fine, and others I was convinced that this was the end.

Everything was confusion, I realized that there was something "extra" in the environment, and if there was not, he created it, I did not know then that I was facing a narcissist who presented himself as a great savior in any situation, he always got people to admire him, he lived in a bubble, a mirage.

I TOOK OFF THE ROLE OF VICTIM

Because of the hope of a change, I focused on rescuing a lost love and the one who lost was me and I hurt myself more than necessary.

I allowed it, I have to assume my responsibility and take off the band of victim, no one can hurt you if you do not allow it. Out of self-denial, you put yourself as a target, it is true, even animals see this.

Let me tell you the story of when I saw it happen with my pets. We came home from a party, it was about two o'clock in the morning, I left the door open and Niko, my dog, got out. When he saw me walking after him, he started to walk down the street. He saw me behind him and walked even more for another block. I went back to get Nala, my other dog, so she would come with me. With Nala we went to look for him. We found Niko and he waited for us, but when we got close, he ran. It was very cold, I was still wearing high heels, and we had already walked a long way. Nala suddenly turned around and went back towards the house, but I was worried that Niko would be stolen. I insisted to Nala to turn back, but she didn't listen to me, she walked faster and never turned around. I shouted to Nala

"Come here!", but she walked faster, and I had to follow her because I didn't want to be alone. I turned around, saw Niko, and said to myself "well, if someone steals you, that's your fault." When Niko realized that we were no longer following him, he ran until he caught up with us. I looked at Nala and thought to myself: "this one is a real dama" and I laughed, and we arrived home together very tired.

Everything in this life teaches us a life lesson. With our insecurity, we give power to those who feel very sure of us.

ONE NAIL DOES NOT DRIVE OUT ANOTHER NAIL, IT DRIVES IT IN DEEPER.

No, I'm not going to look to anyone for comfort, or think that one nail pulls out another nail, rather it sinks it deeper.

Because you have not come out of an emotional conflict with one person and you already got involved with another, this will only create a whirlpool of emotions. If by itself, it is difficult to decipher oneself, now deciphering two people would be even more complex, getting into this whirlpool where the force will drag you, you will not be able to stop it, it will lead you to madness.

When we started our relationship, it was very special, because that love was spontaneous, it was as if we had known each other all our lives, we could talk for hours and hours without getting bored, we enjoyed being together. Personally, I think that the person who will accompany you as a couple is sent to you by God with a purpose.

The mentality that one nail pulls out another nail does not convince me, because no one person is a substitute for another. To start another relationship, you have to heal the wounds left by the previous relationship, otherwise you will make the same mistakes. We are repetitive people of habits and in our mind, habits are formed that are established in the subconscious, these go out to rule a reality, that's why you have to be healthy and sure to start a new relationship.

I have never been able to do things, if I don't have the conviction in my soul, this is something that I have always kept in me, to give myself to another person just because I like it doesn't make sense, just for pleasure instead of filling your life, it empties it.

STUCK IN THE PAST

When I realized that
I was stuck in the past
I ran to my present

and suddenly I found myself
with portraits in my hands
that weighed a lot
and I could no longer carry them,

the weight of the photos
pushed me back,
I almost lost my balance.
To get out of there,
I had to let go.
I "let go" of each one of those memories
that day they were joy,
tenderness and passion.
They are memories
and nothing more,
they have to stay in the past.

IT TAKES TWO TO LOVE

Accepting that you are not interested in me,
that you are distancing yourself from me,
that you don't care about my feelings

and the pain that my eyes show when I see you,
that you ignore everything,
that hurt me to the bottom of my soul
and woke me up to reality.

I know that the love
I had for you
made me hope
and I tried to rescue you
thinking that you were wrong,
I wanted you to value the life
we had made together,
that we were a beautiful family
and that we had been a couple like few others,
enviable, but in the end, nothing worked.
So, ؟what went wrong?
؟How did we get here?

There were many warning signs and I ignored them, and yes, I saw them! I noticed them but I didn't give them any importance because I "trusted in love" I trusted that my love was unique and special, true, unbreakable, that nothing and no one could break it! and yes, it broke, all my attempts were in vain and I realized that to love you need two and to fight for a relationship, one is not enough.

He had already gotten out of my boat and did not row with me, I rowed alone and only went around in the same circle, I was waiting for him to take the other oar so that both of us would reach the shore and that never happened.

I reflected and said: ¡ no more! ¡I've given too much to this relationship! ¡I can't take it anymore! I took the two oars and rowed towards a new horizon where I could see that the darkness was already dissipating and I saw how little by little the sun was coming out, slowly and brightly filling with energy and hope for a new dawn.

You realize that it is a relief to let go. I had to go on, to keep on living because there is always someone who needs you, your presence alone makes them happy and one of them is you yourself.

A SPECIAL MESSAGE

I watched the couples who were our long-time friends laugh, I saw their happiness and it hurt my soul, I felt the loss of my partner, I felt an intense sadness, I tried to appear normal in front of others and I asked myself ¿why me? it was a question I kept repeating over and over again, ¿why me? what did I do wrong to deserve this?

Out of nowhere, I started reading messages popping up from everywhere that said:

"A big loss is not what it seems, it can be a big gain."

"If he plays to lose you, let him win."

"You are an exquisite wine that not everyone knows how to appreciate."

"He doesn't deserve your love."
"Let it go, let him go, life has something else in store for you that will surprise you."

"God wants to give you a special gift."

"Have faith."

"Dry your tears, the pain will pass."

"You have done the right things. God knows what you deserve."

"God heard your plea".

"This is the answer of what you have been asking for so much."

"Life has to take you away from there, because you already served, you did your work and you did it well, that's why God will compensate you."

"Everything has its time, today you cry, but tomorrow you will laugh."

"On the way you will meet people with the same value as you, and by the vibration, you will recognize them."

This went on for quite a while, it would pop up and I'd read the same thing over and over again. I looked at it with amazement at first, but from seeing these messages, the idea entered my mind and heart, I was amazed, I said to myself *"[1]so, does God know this?"* I was amazed and said "*Does God know what has happened*? ؟ *Does He want me out of this relationship*?" I felt like someone was taking me out of a labyrinth, for the first time, I felt that there was something else, that I was not alone. A phrase came to my mind "*The universe is watching you.*" It was guiding me out of this relationship. My time with this person was over and I had to let go and let go. For the first time I felt relief.

---

[11] Belifer You Tube Channel

FAITH

I had to have faith. What is faith: It is the certainty that you are going to get what you want. Imagine it, feel it and take it for granted, you will create an energy that surrounds you and connects with the supreme being that makes things happen.

We cannot do it alone, the emotional burden overwhelms us and faith is the only thing that keeps us afloat, think and decree that everything is going to be fine, have faith.

KARMIC COUPLES

The promise "for life" is very romantic.

Sometimes, that person you fall in love with and then marry, is not always the one who accompanies you for the rest of your life. That partner is called a karmic partner.

A karmic relationship is the coexistence with a partner who will appear in your life to teach you something that you have not been able to learn when you learn it, you transcend it, and the relationship ends because the lesson has been learned.

Between karmic couples, there can be a physical attraction and a lot of chemistry. With this type of couples, a deal is made where they will teach you to live the worst of hell, you will face disappointments, loneliness, sadness, material, and spiritual challenges; in the spiritual challenges you will be confronted with the loss of yourself, because it makes you doubt everything you took for granted.

They are very skillful to get what they want from you, they know you better than you know yourself because they are always watching you, and they know your vulnerabilities to push the button, they know how to approach you when they want something from you, if you don't want to fall, you have to have your antennas working with everything.

A few years ago, I studied hypnotherapy, that science encompasses past life therapy.

I interviewed with a master in the subject: (circa YouTube channel group) we talked, and I learned a lot from her. At a certain moment she asked me about my life, I told her some specific things. When she gave me a sentence, that I was going to get divorced, because that was my destiny, that my contract with my current partner was going to end...that I should prepare myself....

¡I was stunned! ¡I didn't expect it! This happened years ago, and I did not accept it.

Now that I am writing this, what she predicted to me comes to mind. She told me that being a karmic being in someone's life is extremely hard, because its mission is to give you a life lesson, which will produce in your life a turn that you can't even imagine.

I BELIEVED EVERYTHING YOU SAID

You took advantage of me,
of my innocence,
I believed everything you told me.
¡So many deceptions, so many lies!

When you realize it, you become "furious with yourself" and wonder how I could have been so deluded, how did I realize it until now?

Living with a liar is the most depressing and stressful thing you can experience because of his selfishness; he always has a justification that makes you doubt yourself even if you have the evidence in hand. When he is exposed and without justification, he gets angry, and you have to keep quiet so that it doesn't get out of control.

There were so many lies that I had not noticed them, I was so used to their presence, that when I saw them in front of me it was as if a blindfold fell from my eyes and a revelation came to my mind. I began to analyze them one by one, and I saw the betrayal, the lies over and over again. I saw that person, I had her in front of me, and suddenly all her secrets were revealed, and behind the secrets, a reality that paralyzed me.

THE TRUTH ALWAYS COMES OUT

He is the best actor you can find, he has made an art of lying and for everything he has a way out, a perfect answer, for him, rules are not rules. Everything could be broken.

Oh, woe to the women who think that a liar can change. At first, we all believe that this is possible, but over time, you realize that it is easier for him to change you... but for another woman.

I felt a shiver run through my whole body and the feeling I felt for him was one of total disappointment and disillusionment. That love I once felt for him was over, dissipated, broken. It was completely over.

I no longer cared what he said or did, I didn't care, everything about him was a lie, I didn't care to listen to him, it was as if that person no longer existed for me.

SLAVERY

All human beings are born free, equal in dignity and rights, deserving of loyalty, respect, and esteem.

We have seen many movies where people have been captured and detained against their will, and it is terrible. To live a life in slavery! How helpless to see them chained hand and foot with the desire to show up and set them free.

That is what we can see, but there is another more terrible slavery that many people have suffered at some point in their lives and that is emotional slavery. This happens in every kind of relationship, but more in the sentimental one, because we do not know how to love without respecting the freedom of the other: we should be loyal at all times, respect the rights of the partner to be, to feel and to decide.

You decide to be in a relationship and no one else.

When you are not clear, you deceive and hook the partner to your whims and will.

What you don't know, is that cheating makes you a slave of your own actions, to cover up a lie, you have to make it up constantly, until this becomes a snowball that you can no longer stop, creating anxiety, frustration and guilt. Resulting in a personality disorder.

HE CAPTURES YOU IN HIS EMOTIONAL CAGE

The unfaithful is a very intelligent person, observant, calculating, manipulative and good actor.

He knows perfectly your moods and knows how to handle them, any change of attitude is alarming for him, to let you discover his maneuvers or his game.

He is constantly probing how much you know about him, his environment, friends, opinions, all information is valuable. If he sees something that does not add up and has any suspicion of having been discovered, he reaffirms himself as the man concerned about his family and more about you. He is more attentive and intimate with you, he is more affectionate, the details come back, the family days, he keeps you happier than ever and if you had a doubt, it is dispelled. At the end you say to yourself: I imagined it, I'm the crazy one.

He achieved his goal of putting you inside his emotional cage, the very idea of thinking that you can do the same thing he does, of feeling what he feels when he cheats, he can't stand it and he can't let anyone take away the woman who belongs to him, who gives him value and unconditional love to his life.

If the wife, tired of his misdeeds, no longer allows herself to be captivated, does not give in to his love game of reconquest after a slip, and applies indifference, and if she starts listening to romantic music, starts singing, this change of attitude is projected on him and turns into panic, the torment drives him crazy with jealousy, because he feels that his wife is with another man! he cannot stand this!

Oh, because you can't do the same as him!

He begins to observe and investigate more closely. This is the torment of the unfaithful! The projection of his obsessive mind by his very attitudes and behaviors that he knows. This is also an internal fear of losing his wife and makes him see attitudes that may be part of his imagination: "if I do it, everyone can do it", and this makes the relationship very difficult, almost unbearable.

This happened in my relationship, I did not understand his sudden distrust, and I, being naive, did not know what was going on. When someone is so distrustful, it is because they are doing something distrustful.

There was a time when, in a very subtle way, he would initiate a probing conversation, to find out about my activities, where and with whom I went out, my schedule, he knew my movements. He always knew how to move so that I would not notice anything.

Generally, women, when they are in a marriage, are very predictable and almost always have the same routine.

Tip: My friend, I suggest you find something new to do every day, so he will never figure you out so easily and will always wonder where you are.

OBSERVE

My friend from high school always told me, “observe, observe, observe and you’ll see your truth so you can find your peace.” I would respond “I don’t know what you are saying” ¡I don’t understand you! I see everything normal.”

She told me again, observe very carefully and calmly, observe, you are seeing what you created, your projection, your truth, see from the outside, everything that is inside the whirlpool is apparently calm, you need to go out and see from a different point of view to see reality. When you realize the reality, when you are outside the center of the hurricane, everything is completely different.

Go outside the emotion and with a neutral perspective, analyze how you act, how he acts, decipher and you will find the truth. In the end, from so much observing, I found myself, and I discovered my emotion, what was guiding me to act as I had been acting for so many years.

IDEALISTIC PROJECTIONS FADE AWAY

I wanted a home of harmony, peace, and love. At the same time, I wondered: ¿did I want protection? ¿ an ideal? ¿did I want to create what I didn't have with my parents? ¡Oh, something different! I think I finally figured it out!

Definitely, for him, the relationship had no value. At first it did, but then something changed. He played the role of the condescending husband, the one I wanted to see. There comes a moment when you realize, it's all a comedy, it's like doing a complete 360-degree turn... waking up to reality.

The idealistic projections fade away and you have to reinvent yourself, it takes a lot of effort, but in the end, you come back to your center to have a full, real life.

Another of the projections that stops the woman is not to break the relationship because of the helplessness of the children, the projection of the mother worried about the children is a reality, when sometimes it is the children in many of the occasions that ask the mother not to stand it anymore.

I LEARNED TO LAUGH IN THE STORM

When I was in the deepest pain because of my marriage breakup, I avoided all the people around me for a long time. All invitations were turned down because I didn't feel in the mood to be around people. Then one day, I read a paragraph that said, "*Your soul is sad and in pieces inside, you have to know how to be, to live together and to laugh*", this touched my heart.

I understood the sentence and I made an effort to analyze and learn to separate my frustration and feelings for my well-being. I knew that there were situations that had to be resolved in a long time and I had a goal, an end that had to come, and, in the meantime, I had to continue living, I focused on investing my time in productive things and in what I could solve, I did not pay attention to the sadness, and sometimes, suddenly I felt anxiety, but I did not pay attention to it and ignored it, I focused on what was around me to enjoy the moment.

I didn't talk about what was happening to me, ¿for what? there was no point in talking about something that I wanted to be distracted from, I had to create something new for myself, I didn't want to make a circus out of my private life, or talk bad about my partner and create morbidity to be people's material, and that people would be entertained at my expense.

There is a phrase out there, "*if you want to be respected it starts with you, respect your privacy and don't put it in anyone's mouth.*"

I began to create peace, with peace comes calm, with calm comes tranquility and with it the joy of continuing to live.

MY HIGH SCHOOL FRIENDS

God put me with the right people at the right time. When I entered high school, I had three close friends. I stopped seeing them when I immigrated to the United States. When I went to Mexico, I always wanted to look for them. Due to time constraints, I put it off until later and never did it, until one day I decided to and coordinated with my friend, the poet, who I never lost contact with (because she lived near my house) and we went to look for them where I remembered they lived, but everything had changed, the streets where we passed were closed and it was a labyrinth.

We were lost! We went back to the starting point, which was the school, and from there we calculated how many streets it would take to get to where we thought the location might be. So, we drove around in the car, we made many turns, and we didn't get anywhere, so we decided to walk in the middle of the streets. Suddenly I remembered that we crossed a river when I accompanied her home, and we started looking for the river, but we couldn't find it. We asked around and they told us that it was piped, so we traced three possible streets she could live on and started knocking door to door until we found her.

During the three years we were together we laughed at everything and at the same time at nothing, we helped each other unconditionally, it was a very strong magical bond, we protected each other, we supported each other and never reproached each other for anything, we did get annoyed on occasion, but we never fought or distanced ourselves, we were a team of love and harmony. When we met it was as if we had never stopped seeing each other even though so much time had passed, the connection was intact, I felt appreciated, it was an unconditional friendship.

Being in the process of a divorce I felt unconditionally supported by them, no matter what I said they would not judge or reproach me, on the contrary, they were very understanding with me, the support I needed so much came back, especially my philosophical friend who was always there for me at any time, we talked and analyzed very complicated situations that I could not have talked with anyone. This helped me to decipher, analyze and restructure many beliefs and realities that were there in my mind without being able to touch them. I dared, I began to talk about what really scared and hurt me, what paralyzed me with fear and there my friend with her wisdom and reflection gave me her point of view as a friend and with a philosophical approach that made me see realities that I could not see alone.

Now I understand why a dentist cannot remove a tooth.

Every person has an innate gift that is in your life with a purpose, I call them Angels on the road. In my life, God has given me angels, and these are my high school friends.

I appreciate them with all my soul, knowing how to be unconditional friends when you need them the most is pure gold; giving that time, words of encouragement and above all, not judging, this is invaluable.

WHERE CODEPENDENCY BEGINS

A woman does not abandon the man she loves, on the other hand, a man "does abandon the woman he claims to love" (a female convict told me).

The woman represents unity, she unites everything, she envelops it with the magic of her essence, she gives it color, flavor, her cadence, she is a living creation. The woman in love unites with the man she loves and forms a unique energy. *One complements the other and the other complements the one.*

For me this is love.

¿Where does codependency begin? ¿ in not knowing how to let go when the other person does not love you? The logical thing would be to let go and walk away but not all human beings have that logic ¿Who can leave a relationship without pain? ¿Someone who did not give himself emotionally in that relationship. ¿Someone who did not feel. Who lived in a false relationship to leave just like that?

When we fall in love, it awakens a unique, beautiful feeling that we connect to our senses by giving ourselves to love, we idealize it, and we expect to be loved deeply. When we lose this feeling, we mourn the loss and there is terrible suffering. When people say, "Get over it already!" Truly, one wants to get over it! the mind tells you to do it, but, however, the heart wants to die.

Usually, no one knows or understands how to "let go" of someone you love or loved, the love does not stop in you, just because the other person stopped loving you. Love is still there.

When you feel abandoned, disappointment comes, and then you know there is a loss and loneliness create a reality that you have to face sooner or later, and there comes your reality and you realize that love is over. Codependency is handled as an attachment, and yes, it is an attachment when you love, want and long to be twenty-four hours a day with your partner, you think about him from dawn to dusk. It can be handled as an addiction, and yes, it is an addiction, it is because you become addicted to everything that is related to it, yes, we have all gone through it in our life, it lowers your performance totally, to zero, then you realize that you have an excessive dependency and you have to focus and balance, but all people who have loved have experienced this type of behavior. Codependency begins in not knowing how to let go when someone is no longer there for you.

NALA AND NIKO

When I felt sad, I would lock myself in my bedroom, tormented by memories of very happy moments, which turned into dark and gloomy thoughts and emotions that came and went in my anguished mind until I was exhausted. I would lie down for hours without moving, alone, sad.

One day, I got out of bed and stumbled upon Nala, my little dog. The first time I thought it was strange, the second time I thought it was a coincidence and the other times I realized that she was there for a purpose, because she slipped in to be there with me like a best friend, who says nothing, but her presence was enough. She would be there for hours and hours, lying next to my bed; I would look at her and she would see me with such a sad look that it puzzled me. She was there, all the time looking out for me.

Nala came into our lives when my daughter was turning sixteen a friend of her told her about the dog as a gift for her birthday; but she warned her that she had been with a dog trainer and that she had been badly mistreated. In order not to give her to a shelter, she was taken from one family to another, they didn't want her because they thought she was too much responsibility, so, lastly, she was temporarily taken care of by a family, but they had her in the yard in the rain and cold so she would leave, and the sad and muddy dog stayed in a corner, until my daughter and I brought her to our house.

From that moment on, Nala looked super happy, jumping up and down with joy and happiness, and little by little she adapted to the family.

As she had been abused, every time we talked to her, she would freeze and pee from fear, but every time my ex-husband came home from work, Nala would get up from wherever she was and go out to the yard to avoid him. After a while, she did not go out anymore, she would go to a corner and from there she would watch us, little by little she would get closer.

My children have always been very affectionate with their father and he with them, Nala would watch in amazement how they played with each other, time went by and she got closer to the door especially at the time when we could hear the car when he arrived, then she was the first one to receive him and she was so happy she would go crazy with joy.

Nala looked lonely, so we decided to find her a dog to keep her company. We saw an ad about an Akita dog being put up for adoption in San Diego and went with my daughters and Nala to meet him. When we arrived, the owner showed us two Akitas dogs, one with the same coat as Nala and the other was white. We walked with the dog that looked like Nala and he didn't look at her, nor did she look at him.

Then we walked with the white dog, he became very restless wanting to get close to Nala, we were afraid he would bite her, but nothing like that happened, on the contrary, when he got close to her, he jumped with joy, and when they were walking, he hugged and kissed her. I had never seen anything like that, it seemed incredible to me that a dog would act like that, I realized that there was an attraction, a very strong chemistry, a crush between animals, he looked like Pepe Le Pew (the skunk in the cartoon who fell in love with a cat who accidentally painted her tail) and I thought it was nice to share this story. Nala allowed herself to be courted.

Nala approached my daughter. She stood in front of her and gave her a kiss on the cheek, my daughter understood what Nala wanted and said, "Nala wants the white dog" and I asked her "how do you know it? "Didn't you see that Nala kissed my cheek?" Nala said to me "buy it for me, buy it from me, buy it from me" and if I hadn't seen it, I wouldn't have believed it, a dog super in love, and I said, "this is love at first sight." So, we brought him home.

Already in the car I realized that the dog was huge, and I was very worried about how we were going to educate the dog, Nala was already trained, she knew how to live with us, she knew how to go to the bathroom, she was very discreet, polite and cheerful; incredibly, she gradually educated Niko, our new doggy member.

The love between Nala and Niko has brought a lot of balance to the atmosphere of the house and I felt it very present in the days when I needed it the most. With the breakup of the marriage, I felt a lot of tension, uncertainty, environmental chaos, something that makes you so tense that you feel that at any moment it explodes and becomes madness, I saw them, and they approached and gave love to each one of us, as if they knew what the soul needed at that moment, "unconditional love."

At that time, I was not inclined to anything, I felt like a leaf from a tree that falls into a river and is carried away by the current, I did not put resistance or attention to anything or anyone. It was like going into survival mode. One day at a time (song: Yesenia Flores), of just living without expecting anything from anything. I wouldn't go near my children because I didn't want them to see how devastated I was, but Nala and Niko were there, distracting and attracting their attention. They helped a lot to maintain the love, harmony and calm that once existed in that family nucleus and that my children needed so much.

When I ended the relationship, I left my bedroom and settled in the living room. I felt lost, I couldn't find my place, I missed my bed. The couches, even though they make a bed, are very padded and very warm, so I put a mattress flush on the floor "I didn't want to go into my children's rooms because I wanted to respect their privacy and I also wanted to have time to be alone" and analyze my situation.

The ceiling in the living room is very high, cool and spacious, although I felt comfortable, I couldn't curl up, let alone sleep. I had seen a documentary about caves and caverns around the world, and suddenly I found myself in a cold cave alone, with a hole in my heart. That day, it was one of the moments when I have felt loneliness in all its being. The next day was the same. One day I felt different, I was able to sleep, and I felt curled up, I woke up rested and happy, suddenly I heard some snoring, and it was Niko, he was next to me. From then on, every night he slept around me, I never felt lonely again.

I found a message that said that dogs are an energetic protector, that they absorb unbalanced vibrations from the environment and they in turn clean themselves by giving unconditional love to the family. There are animals in the animal shelter waiting to be adopted and give you unconditional love and support when we need it most.

Nala and Niko got sick continuously during the time I had the crisis in my marriage, when I realized this, I put more dedication and began to care for them more. As they took care of me and the family, I put healing stones (gemstones) that purify the energy, I made herbal oils and sprays to balance them, and their vitality returned. We went for constant walks, especially in places where there is a lot of vegetation, so they have a connection with the earth and stay healthy.

¡What an experience! ¿Who would have thought that dogs would help me through this time in my life? I learned to value nature and its divine gifts more and to respect and value pets that come to us with a purpose; we need them more than they need us.

When they feel bad, they come to me with their sad look and with their attitude they make themselves understood, they tell me with their look that they do not feel well, it is like telepathy because I feel their expression and I attend them with my home remedies.

My daughters laughed at me, they told me "¿and what does Nala tell you? ¿how does she tell you?" "manta (manita in Spanish) I feel bad" and they laughed, but in the end, they were convinced. Even though they take the dogs to the vet it takes a long time to recover and with my remedies it is faster, and at the end they tell me "mom, Nala is not feeling well, ¿can you cure her?" and Nala with her look tells me yes.

My daughter suggests me to make a line of holistic products for pets, ¿what do you think?

If you want one of the products that I put on my dogs, send me an email.

sanacionparamismascotas@gmail.com

I KNEW THE LONELINESS

I couldn't find myself. I felt myself with my whole being, with no one, it was as if I had discovered myself for the first time.

From the moment you are born you have your parents who are there for you, your siblings, friends, then husband and children. Suddenly, that which sustains you is no longer there *(husband)* . All the affections I knew were there, but they could not give me a hand, because, even if they gave it to me, I would not accept it.

When they asked me if I needed something, I felt their words were empty. When they wanted to support me, I would walk away. Now I analyze it and I think that it is the soul that wants to be alone with you and you have never allowed that encounter of recognition, rapport and belonging. The being, you, and her, then you see the reality of your rebirth, alone.

The hardest experiences of life, you have to go through alone, and that no one, absolutely no one can help you, it is you and only you facing life, so raw, so real, without anesthesia. When that experience happens and you overcome it, then you know what life tastes like, and you can enjoy it and laugh, because you have reconciled with yourself, because you had to let go of all the comfort you knew to be you, a unique being.

And you know that you only have yourself and nothing else, you are born alone, and you die alone. One day, I saw a Mexican movie that moved me a lot when I saw a phrase in the movie that said: "You will not have arrived until you have lost everything", now I think about it again and yes, that is right.

NO MORE EMOTIONAL ATTACHMENTS, I LET GO OF THE BACKPACK

I felt lost, I thought one thing, felt another, and did another.

I am not going to hurt myself anymore, no more longing, no more going to the past. He was not where I was looking for him, his soul, his essence, his illusions, and passions were no longer here with me; I did not hear any more romantic music to remind me of him, I did not see pictures where we were in love and I had to keep my wedding picture where I would not see it anymore.

I avoided all emotion; I wasn't going to give emotion a chance to wallow.

One day, I thought one thing, and other days, totally another. When I saw my wedding photo, I felt a thread of illusion that was about to burst, and I tried to hold on to it! *I said to myself, how am I going to leave this that was so beautiful! I had to fight,* and I got hooked, I submerged myself in a well of emotions where I sank and I was impregnated with pain, disappointment for what was inside and that I did not want to see, I covered it with a veil, from which I had a hard time getting out, and when I finally got out, I came out all disillusioned, torn to pieces.

I would say one thing, think another and do something else; more and more time would pass, and life was filling me with bitterness. I had to align them, between saying, doing, and thinking. I was going to base my decision to end this relationship that was hurting me so much, I was not going to allow doubt to cross my mind once again. Lots of memories, emotions, but I wasn't going to let it sway me anymore. From that moment on, every time I remembered something, I did not allow it to alter my senses, I did not pay attention to it, nor did I put resistance, and I did not try to avoid it, because the more you want to avoid it, the more it persists, I was firm in not giving my feelings or time to anything related to it.

The mind plays tricks on you, suddenly you start to hear in your mind a song of memory where you are transported in the time of memories, when this happened, I tried to pay attention to something else. One emotion would bring another emotion and then another.

"Educate your mind and you will be free" and that is what I did, educate my mind to have peace and I let go of the emotional backpack. Look for the title of the blue book on how to handle emotions.

ADMIRATION AND RESPECT

When you lose admiration and respect for your partner you lose everything, you do not care about his beliefs, impositions, opinions, his lack of love, you ignore everything, I no longer get angry or bother me what he does, says or thinks, I no longer make dramas.

He realized this, the challenges were stronger every day because he felt ignored, he did everything to get my attention and now he created the dramas, he wanted to unbalance me at all costs, but I had more strength and tolerance, I could handle my emotions without any outburst, and I no longer fell into his psychological traps.

Everything he said to me was analyzed and I answered him without any emotional inclination, the emotion had made me wallow, martyred me and I was not going to let him anymore, this unbalanced him more than me, because he no longer had me in his hands, I got out of his control and this hurt him to the bone.

¡THE SITUATION REPEATS OVER AND OVER AGAIN! IS IT A SIGNAL TO RELEASE?

I felt very sad and distressed, the fights came back and so did his lack of interest.

You know your partner perfectly well, you know when he is lying, when he is having affairs... your instinct tells you. Likewise, he knew me, and he knew I could tell when he was starting a new relationship. I always went to church and prayed, I thought that women were home wreckers and that they wanted to take him away from me and I wasn't going to allow that, I had to save my marriage!

It was a torment, I don't know why I was so stupid, when I told someone, I trusted about my situation they would say: "¡fight for your marriage!

¡he is your husband! ¡ he is the father of your children! ¡You have a marriage of many years! ¡it should not be thrown away! ¡and that a woman is going to take everything you worked for! ¡What you're going through, happens to all marriages! ¡That is how they get at this age! ¡They feel young and want to conquer whoever is in front of them!"

"¡Ah! ¿so, it is not as tragic as I think it is, I'll let it go one more time?" I thought so. ¡But he grabbed it as a sport! the situation became untenable, ¡he knew he was going to give everything for the marriage, he was absent and thought I was going to be waiting for him and still be the same self-sacrificing and suffering woman! The situation made me tired, and I saw myself in the same scene over and over again.

I asked myself ¿why do I have to be going through this? Deep in my conscience I knew what I had to do, your intuition screams the truths in your face, but you don't want to hear it, you don't listen to it, if you did, you would avoid a lot of suffering and waste of time.

I saw a message that told me, *"God already gave you many signs to let go of that toxic partner, if you don't do it, then God will do it his way and get ready because then, you will know what suffering is, let go or let go, because God doesn't want that partner for you."*

A therapist told me that situations are repeated until you give them a solution. Another message that appeared said that *God knows that you are not happy and puts the same situation to enter in conscience, you free yourself.*

A friend who attended church one day told me that she thought that the weakness of men was women and that is why the temptation presented itself and overcame them, so she decided that whenever she could, she would go to church to pray that temptation would move away from her husband, and she told me: *"I don't know why God doesn't hear my prayers.*

SETTING LIMITS

Infidelity is felt, as well as in the environment, he is not the same as before, all the red lights go on and you see signs of infidelity.

People prefer not to know. Ignore so as not to suffer or face reality. They don't want to wake up out of fear, and fear paralyzes you and you don't know what to do or how to act. You think that this will pass, and no, it does not. Now your partner has a more intimate and deeper connection with another person, and what you wanted to avoid turns against you, you feel that the sky is falling on you, his detachment and lack of love are your worst torment.

You could have faced it before it caused so much pain and put a solution to it with cunning, intelligence, firmness and giving you your courage. Everything you could have done loses meaning and courage, he realized somehow that you knew about his infidelity and did nothing, and instead of stopping, he gave it everything because he knew he was not going to lose you.

This is what a friend told me, to which I asked her, "why didn't you do anything?" To which she replied, "*I was afraid, I thought he was going to get tired and in the end he would come back.*"

BE CAREFUL WITH MONEY

Money is the first thing to flee when a marriage is in crisis. When a married man goes out of the fold, you begin to realize that you no longer receive birthday gifts, anniversaries, special details. A drastic cut in extra expenses for meals out, outings, and worst of all, the paycheck no longer comes home the same; even though expenses like the ones mentioned above are no longer being made.... Where are you spending your money? ... I think it is time to review your bank statement.

Every couple has their own method of organizing their finances, in my case, we as a married couple never talked about having a plan on how to manage the household money, big mistake!!! and it gets worse when the family goes into crisis.

Comfort and blind trust in the couple generates stupidity in the woman's financial world.

ECONOMIC ABUSE

Personally, I had no special savings for myself, I worked all day at home and dedicated 100% to my children and him, there was trust.

The problem started when he changed and took everything he could. At first, I did not notice, every day he said that he spent more and thus the expenses of the house were bad because I did not confront the situation and sit down to make accurate accounts of what came in and out of the house, he was taking more and more power over the money and began to tell me that I did not make payments on time. That was a lie, which was a perfect excuse for him to take control of the management of everything.

I knew he was determined to take everything he could from the house. I was devastated, heartbroken and sad and didn't want to deal with it, so I let him take everything he could.

He asked me to work because he wanted me to pay my expenses, because according to him he had no obligation to pay me anything and he always checked the refrigerator to see if he had bought extra food, and if something went bad, he would get very angry. If he saw something new, he got upset and complained to me because I bought it, this was the most terrible and you do not have to wait for one to reach those extremes of having to endure financial abuse.

This gave me a life lesson and unfortunately one reacts very late, at this point, I had to face the situation, when I realized it, put a remedy on it, but out of fear, I kept quiet and lost more. In the end the situation reached an intolerable point.

My grandmother who is in heaven was left a widow and always saved her money, she was self-sufficient, and she told me, "*mija, save your money, don't spend everything, think about the future*" and I heard her, but she didn't; was very organized in my expenses

A woman should always have savings for herself, in case of emergency, in case of divorce or widow, because nothing is certain in this life, only what one does for oneself.

In an interview with a writer who was very successful, I heard her say that she was a woman abandoned by her husband and left her young children, she had a very difficult financial situation, but she had the illusion of one day getting out of there, she dreamed of traveling around the world alone, she made up her mind to save a dollar a day, without touching her savings no matter what, when her children grew up enough to be independent, she went to travel alone with the money that she had saved, after so much struggle she made her dream come true. Elizabeth Gilbert's memoir
Eat, Pray, Love Chronicles the journey of self-discovery.

ECONOMIC VIOLENCE AGAINST WOMEN

It takes away all financial resources, you feel kidnapped in a relationship without physical chains, your emotional chains are stronger. One looks for the aggressor outside, but he is inside in the bosom of your family, this is more difficult to notice because you hide it and hide it very well. You endure abuse out of shame, and you constantly tell yourself, "*This can't be passing me*!", you are afraid of what they will say.

Sometimes you confront him by telling him how you feel about his attitude, he responds that it is not true, that it is not like that, that you interpreted it wrong. This type of abuse makes love go into the background, and although love does not dissolve from one minute to the next, yours-with so much abuse-dissolved.

You know that you must end the relationship and act without emotion, be objective, assertive for your release.

WOMEN'S ECONOMY

For women, saving should be a primary practice to move forward, because nothing is safe, a marriage does not buy the security of anything or anyone.

Likewise, statistics show that men die before women, even though women have their children, they will always be conditioned to what others want for not having solvency.

One day, I met a woman who liked to gamble in Vegas and one day she was told about investing her money in stocks. She liked the suggestion and began to invest a few cents, taking it as a hobby. She learned little by little, until she became an expert in the subject, and with this she earned a lot of money.

Because when a woman becomes an expert in something she likes, she turns it into gold. She inherited her children during her lifetime, she stayed in her own house, she had three people who took care of her until her death, she planned everything very well.

I have always said, and I passionately believe that women move the economy of the home and the world. That is why I tell you, once again, that we are the ones who move the economy. If the husband wants to buy something he asks us and if we say no, it is "no", and if we approve it is done, the husband is not going to throw a fight with his wife for a disagreement.

Here in the United States the woman dresses the man, buys him a gift shirt, and pants every month and some shoes and dresses him as she wants, gives what she wants to eat to the whole family, pays the bills, moves everything in the home.

There is no turning point in this matter, the woman must act with intelligence and create a good economic support by saving and spending with intelligence.

The best heritage you can create during a marriage, or at any time in your life, is investing in a home. In the event that you do it within marriage with your partner, this will not only give stability to the home, but will also make you feel supported and calm because you have something that belongs to you and that will later belong to your children.

Now, it often happens that many of us do not give importance to this and money disappears like water in our hands, A Colombian friend told me: "*Buy a house*" and I told her no because I was going to go to Mexico, then she replied: *You Mexicans always have your suitcase at the door, and you don't do anything, you're not here or there."*

I thought about it and I identified with what she said because I felt without stability because there was no sense of belonging for me here or there, because I felt deep sadness because I always longed for what I had left behind, among that my home, but not I saw that I could create something like that again until I finally had my home, I already felt that I belonged to this place and I had the confidence to interact in the community and became part of it.

?WHAT CAN YOU DO?

It sounds like a movie title, well it is, and I liked the title and the story.

A young woman with two small children, the husband goes out for cigarettes and never comes back. She, in desperation, begins her search, discovering that the husband has a lover, a young man who is in Acapulco.

The abandoned wife is left alone with no money and no idea what to do. She has a neighbor who takes care of the children. She sought out her best friend who owned a funeral home. While waiting for her to receive her, she went to sit in one of the funeral parlors and there she had a crying fit and fainted from the anguish she was going through. The family of the deceased wondered who she was and why she was crying in such pain. The deceased's family starts the rumors. The friend receives her and tells her about her grief, cries,

and cries and asks her for a job. The friend asks her: -And you, what do you know what to do? -She answers: - Well, nothing, after I got married, I left everything to take care of the house. The friend says to her: - Think of something you can do well.

- Well, what I know how to do well is to cry, cry and cry.

- To which the incredulous friend says: - Really?

- yes, I cry very well, I even fainted!

- well, you are hired, let's add a weeper to the funeral home packages for their dead![2]

---

[2] Pelicula. Te daria mi vida, pero la estoy usando. Cecilia Suarez

NEGLIGENCE OR DECEPTION

The lack of information and knowledge in contracts, legal processes, insurance company's policies, loans, wills, etc., brings therefore that they are badly processed by negligence of oneself, for not having the papers in order and not being 100% sure that it is correct, creating irreparable losses in families, which

The lack of information and knowledge in contracts, legal processes, insurance companies' policies, loans, wills, etc., brings therefore that they are badly processed by negligence of oneself, for not having the papers in order and not being 100% sure that it is correct, creating irreparable losses in families, which sometimes is very difficult or impossible to repair, and above all to recover and this can lead a family to total ruin.

A family is an institution and has to be a function of society.

This requires having the services and paperwork to have a house, car insurance, life insurance, medical services, schools, purchase of house and property titles etc.

Before starting the divorce process, I obtained all the necessary information that I needed to carry out each step. There were many papers to gather, including the title of the house, in which my name should be as co-owner. I never gave importance to this issue, but when I started the process, I realized that it was something especially important.

When I was already in court processing my divorce, I saw a lady in the line next to me who looked very troubled, I asked her if she was okay and she answered no, that she had just realized that her husband mortgaged the house for $400,000.00 with the house almost paid for, and now she would have to make a monthly payment of $3,000.00 if she wanted to continue to live in the house, when the house was almost paid off.

When my divorce was finished, I review all the legal paper to make sure everything was in order.

Salesmen tell you what you want to hear, but on paper they tell the truth, go through your papers one by one and consult an outside party. Most people procrastinate and are not interested, but when things get complicated, we desperately look for someone to help us solve the problem when we could have avoided it.

In conversations with many people, I was discovering the damage caused by this lack of information, deception, or negligence of themselves for trusting that everything is fine.

No matter what they tell you, seek three different opinions until you are totally convinced that it is the truth.

The following are different stories I have been told about it:

Celia tells: My husband was very sick, but I never thought he was going to die, I canceled a life insurance that paid 200 month in case of death the house would be paid off. I thought I was saving money and suddenly he died, I lost the house because I could afford the payments. Now I have two jobs to pay for a small apartment and completely abandon my children.

In another comment, Marcela says: She had divorced, kept the house, but during the fire season her house was affected and burned completely. Because she had no insurance, she could not rebuild it. Eventually she lost it.

Gloria says: "When my husband died, I found out that my name was not on his life insurance policy. The only names that appeared on that document were his parents' names. By not informing me or interfering in the documents that were important for my protection, I was left with nothing, it had never crossed my mind that my name was not on that life insurance policy. Never take anything for granted.

Nancy comments: I was happy, because as far as I understood it, our house was paid off, but the payment demands kept coming. When I inquired about the loan, it said that the interest was paid and when it was finished, I would start paying off the debt on the house.

¡¡¡ The moneylender cheated on me!!! So many years without seeing the lie and I never asked someone else.

Teresa: My husband never wanted us to buy a funeral arrangement, a little piece of land for when one rests in peace, he always told me not to bring bad luck, when he was ill and was evicted we were a terrible economic crisis, *you cannot even process the pain* for the worry about what you are going to do, I remember leaving the doctor's office I felt so sad and furious with him, at the same time, I told him that he never did what I asked him to do, we spent the money on … I don't even know what?

And now we don't have money for his funeral. I ask him *to tell me which trash you want me to throw you into*?

Juana: we were coming from the doctor, he was weak months before, the doctor just told us that there was no remedy, they had evicted him, I thought and thought, how to get money for a special treatment, but no, we did not have the money, always solving the life of someone else, always lending money that in the end is given away, because… we are here in the United States, they are not going to pay you. And now who is going to pay for this…for this treatment. I was thinking while I am walking slowly. The night was very cold I was tumbling with fear, the street was very dark and dangerous I don´t even know where we where I say to him walk faster, he was walking behind me very slow I told him again mad walk faster. I had a whirlwind of mixed feeling I was very with him because are fights were because he always spends all the money to please people around us, I felt so helpless and turned to see him and said, yes of course, ¡you are going to die soon! later a regretted it, but I felt I was true.

Rosa: My husband died, he fixed everything, I must do the pension procedure and I don't know how I'm going to do it; I don't have any passwords. Now they ask for keys for everything. If I could go back in time, I would ask you to fill in all the data that one should know, if I could, believe me they are months of paperwork for not knowing the correct information.

All these situations are very devastating, so make a list of each procedure that you know is important, check each of the papers and read, if you changed banks, make the change in the account, thousands of dollars are lost, you not realized that you did not change the information and you did not have the contacts registered to contact you, the benefits are lost because the account is canceled. Find out and investigate, above all, that it is correct and in perfect order.

Many of the life penalties are easier to carry with money, so save, save, it is one less anguish.

When you can do things in life, you avoid a great pain for those you leave behind, then there are many losses and regrets, leave everything in writing, so that the beneficiaries know all the information about the assets, in a safe place so that when it is needed, it is there, and you do not want to resurrect the dead.

An uncle bought a piece of land and left it as an investment, he died and the wife forgot the matter, shortly after they went with their family for a walk to remember old times and saw that a road passed through the land, the state had seized it, they went to claim and were told that the government wanted to buy that land and they did everything possible to contact the person who owns this land, they put ads in the newspaper, until the time of the law passed, they could confiscate it and there was nothing that legally could be done to get it back, it hurt them with all their soul because it was hectares of land and it was worth millions.

My grandfather lent some land to his brothers, when my uncles were young, my grandfather died, they forgot about the matter and it was my grandfather's brothers who got the land and now the children are the ones who stayed with an inheritance that did not belong to them.

The most advisable thing is to make a Living Trust, ¿what is a Trust? It is a provision by means of which a testator leaves his inheritance or part of it entrusted to a person so that, in each case or time, he transfers it to another, or invests it in a way that is indicated.

These situations are very devastating, so take every piece of paperwork that matters to you, check it out, get informed and do your research, above all, make sure it is correct and in perfect order.

UNDERSTANDING MY MOOD

One conflict ended and another one began, it was a very exhausting emotional struggle, in which I was overwhelmed to the point of exhaustion, I felt devastated, my soul was in tatters.

One of the last battles I was fighting, I should have faced it and ended it since I realized that the relationship was hopeless. I just had to count the damage and rescue what I could without putting up any resistance, but no!... I prolonged the situation to see if the relationship would recover, since he changed, the relationship was hopeless (his coldness, his blunt attitude and lack of interest was evident that he wanted to break the relationship) But no ¡ The woman does not think or act like that! We suffer for free!

¡I could not find comfort! But encouragement always comes where you least expect it: I went to visit my sister and one of my brothers was at her house visiting, and he was reading a book entitled: *CHRIST AND ME* and he told me: take this book, open it. God has a message for you. I took the book and opened it randomly. The message said: *"My beloved soul, I have seen you crying. Ah, your tears, you are paying dearly for the price of your past mistakes, you never realized that indulging yourself so much was going to cost you so dearly, did you?*

I have forgiven you, but you are suffering for not being able to forget so many scars and memories that you have in your mind and no matter how hard you fight you cannot forget, come here, be docile, I will help you, I need a little humility from you, I need deep simplicity and acceptance to my will, I have allowed you to live all these states of the soul, of a depressive mood so that you can understand others and never judge, so that you can be more docile and understanding at all times, so that you may help through your existence all the souls who, like you, have their souls in tatters, because all of them, my soul, have their souls shattered by so many things that happen to them, that they themselves often provoke by compensations, others by mistakes, that they do not understand that they are hurting themselves, try to grasp your state of mind, do not despair, remember, my grace is enough for you. Be patient, be patient, be in deep prayer and wait for peace to come to you in addition because I can give you everything, as long as you are docile and humble; I want to fill you with my goodness so that you may inundate all those around, but today, those tears do you good, because you are relieving your mistakes; tell those around you that sin always costs tears. Come, most beloved soul, I am going to console you. [3]

From then on, I let things flow and no longer got stuck in the emotions that made me stagnant, frustrated, and paralyzed, which did not allow me to think of solutions and actions that I had to face and execute.

This message gave me peace and so came many more from different sources. I knew I had to make this message known and that is what inspired me to write this book to guide people who are going through a divorce or separation process and know that everything has a solution.

I hope it can help you. God spoke to me and I began to listen to him and to trust him.

---

[3] Libro CRISTO Y YO Anamaria *Rabatte*

FACING FEAR

The dread paralyzed me, I gave myself courage, I faced fear.

When you live with fear, you fear losing, because you are insecure, you feel lost and because you are afraid of not losing, you lose more.

You see fear, you observe it, you feel it, you palpate it, and you realize that you learned it as a child, it was always there, hidden and when you tried something new, it woke up, but I still challenged it and defeated it, accomplishing my goals, now I know, after suffering so much from fear, now I let fear be afraid of me!

Crossing the penumbra of fear, you find the achievements you fought for, and the satisfaction brings you happiness.

A WITHERED SOUL

Attachment with fear "terrible combination for a relationship."

"It changes the attitude of the lover who instead of enjoying and giving the best of himself, is always alert defending his love and is on the defensive so that his great gift is not taken away, this in turn acts and everything that made him fall in love with the partner now begins to take it away so that no one sees those gifts that captivated him one day; he does it little by little without the partner realizing it, and if he realizes it, he justifies it because he does it and thinks he loves her and he does not want anyone to see her and know her qualities."

Yes, I like my high heels, I said to myself after I bought them. They are very high, too high, he said. The dress I loved was too flashy or too short. The hairstyle I wore was for young people. The color I liked was not so nice. I was taking away my tastes for dressing for myself, for doing things for my taste.

So much so, that I realize the loss, until I have been left with nothing of what I was before, but I accept it because it is no longer important what I like, because I no longer have time for that, there are more important things that I must attend to.

I am losing my essence, I feel that something is missing, but I don't know what it is. I no longer smile as I used to, nor do I dare to do fun things, everything I do is in favor of the family. Me, I remain unimportant to everyone.

¡He achieved his goal! that I delegate myself to the background, so he is no longer afraid that someone will captivate me, and I fall in love with someone else, but he doesn't realize that all this is turning me off, I gave more life to him than to me, the energy that flowed in me no longer shone as before, my spirit feels deprived, there is no more food for the spirit. Everything is an obligation for me, it ceases to amaze me, everything seems daily and boring.

When depression arrives, the soul withers, that which made us shine has faded, the admiration he once felt for me has gone, he no longer sought me with his joyful gaze, what captivated him about me vanished, he turned it off himself and punished himself, I no longer make him vibrate and he feels monotonous and bored and knows that something is missing so he goes in search of another person who has a brightness that captivates him just like the one he once turned off.

INFIDELITY

The unfaithful man thinks he is very clever, he thinks he can do anything, he plays on two fronts and is very skilled at handling his wife. He tells the other one the truth, that he is married and must accept it, if not, there is no game.

The other one for convenience accepts because for her it is not a priority, it has no value, it is just a distraction, a hidden relationship. She plays that she loves him, and he supplies her vanity with expensive gifts and attentions, she doesn't mind being submerged to the social annulment, to the hiding, here each one has his well-structured conveniences, it is a deal, it is very easy to dissimulate and follow the game of seduction, which he feels that gives him power until his same game traps him and leaves him uncovered with the wife.

The signs are obvious, his look changes, his attitude is different, it is as if his programming has been changed and he is someone else. What started as a harmless game, ends up being a trap where the hunter ends up being hunted.

IT'S NOT LOVE, IT'S OBSESSION

You beg as if he would pity you, he does not love you.

He doesn't even love himself: he doesn't know what love is. The unfaithful plays with love, plays with the feelings of the one who gives him his attention, thinks only of his desires, what fills him and makes him go out of reality.

The characteristics of an unfaithful person:
-A giver of nothing, demanding everything.
-An unconscious, where the woman is a game and is an object in his hands.
-He will bend the woman with sweetness to fill himself with her, when a novelty appears that fills his taste, they leave without any type of remorse.
-His motto, talk to the woman about love and sincerity until she believes it.

THE WOMAN ENTERS THE SAME GAME

The woman, hurt by so much deceit, chooses to play the same game as him, so she resorts to revenge, and says to herself: "If you like this so much", ¡ let's see what it tastes like! Let's play the same game that everyone plays."

The two enter a game and actions where they use the most sophisticated tricks to deceive each other, they live in an atmosphere of tension, rapture and disaffection, where they are both slaves of their own traps.

Carol felt deceived, she already knew all her husband's tricks. We were sitting in a park and I saw her very thoughtful and I asked her: "what's the matter, you look worried", she answered: "Oscar is already up to his tricks" I replied: "*what a pity*!" and she ended up saying: "*Pity" Ha, ha, he's the one who is going to feel sorry, he hurts me, and I hurt him back twice as much."*

APPEARANCES IN FRONT OF THE FAMILY ENSLAVE YOU

For the sake of appearances and the need to feel loved, you put up with all kinds of abuse that makes you an emotional slave. You get hooked to a harmful emotion and be part of a relationship, even if it is destructive.

You see it as a necessity and social obligation, this makes you act like a slave, because all the time you will be stalking your partner so as not to lose his love, even if it means losing your life.

You do this so as not to feel like a failure in the family environment. At the end of keeping up appearances, the realities cannot be hidden, and, in the end, you end up alone.

They violate your values and primordial rights so as not to lose your relationship, even losing yourself to the point of not recognizing yourself. Don't confuse your need with love, you can enslave yourself to the point of betraying yourself.

The writer (Walter Riso) said that where there is a slave, there will always be a master.

During a television interview of a very well known and loved artist who was talking about her divorce, she looked very devastated. She was explaining what it was like to have suffered the breakup and not accept it because she didn't want to be defeated in front of her family.

Until her son told her, *"Mom, that's enough, you did everything to save the relationship, this is too much for you, accept it, your relationship is over.*" Seeing her son so affected by her, she realized how instead of saving a family, she was sinking it into heartbreak and disappointment.

¿WHY DOES THE PARTNER CHEAT?

There are people who should never have gotten married and started a family, but still, they did. They got engaged! For a while they fell in love with their partner, but life, feelings and emotions moved them in a different direction and their engagement broke down.

They weren't honest, they didn't say anything to anyone, they created a world apart where they only played by indulging their whims. They kept up appearances to belong to the group of friends and family, because they knew that with their ideas and actions they could not be accepted.

I believe that everyone has the right to live what he/she wants and likes with complete freedom, as long as he/she is honest and does not deceive the other person. I find it very cowardly to lie, it's really despicable, to keep a false appearance and still want your partner to admire you. She knows you better than you know yourself and just by looking at you, she knows you are lying.

THEY MAKE THE CONQUEST A WORK OF ART

He thinks it is a disadvantage not to have a graceful physical appearance and believes that no one will accept him as a partner, he analyzes his situation, knows that he has to accentuate his favorable points to be accepted and begins to modify his personality.

He becomes more pleasant, more attentive, more accommodating and begins to train himself to improve his conversation, he begins to read a lot to be more interesting and broaden his cultural horizons, he creates goals in personal achievements. Everything he thinks is a defect, he turns into a quality.

He challenges himself to conquer a girl unattainable for him and, in the end, he succeeds, this calms him down and he goes beyond the limitation and from there to the conquest! The adrenaline that he secretes in the whole process, details, attention is a delight and the taste of the conquest becomes a vice, creating a conqueror with an ego up to the clouds.

I had a friend who said he was very ugly, I didn't see him that way, but he considered himself "the ugly one", he was very nice and funny, that idea was a trauma for him. I asked him, "why do you think that about yourself." He told me that at home he had always heard that he was ugly. You realize how what you get to hear about yourself, a negative comment as a child can traumatize you forever, if you don't know who you are and you don't accept, value and like yourself, ''you can skew your personality drastically."

He, to be accepted, was very detail oriented, kind, and paid a lot of attention to detail. He knew that these qualities are what a woman craves.

He knew that with these qualities he could conquer any woman, he had already created a style of conquest and had made an art out of it.

IS CONDEMNED TO BE A CHEATER

¿Is infidelity (disloyalty) in the genes? You may have heard people say: He came out just like his father, grandfather, uncle, etc. .... or ¡he is the happy eye of the family; it runs in his blood! ¿ What is the reason for this behavior? ¿is it because of the high level of dopamine in the blood? ¿ in the heart? ¿ in the brain? (Dopamine: the hormone that produces pleasure) this makes them more vulnerable.

When they are not in control, their behavior is always inclined to conquest and seduction. These behaviors predominate in character, every time they have an opportunity for conquest, the brain produces a discharge of dopamine making them addicted to pleasure.

[4]Dopamine presents a greater tendency to be unfaithful and more, if this runs in their genetics, which goes from one generation to another, from grandfather, father, son, and now, he is unfaithful.

---

[4] Un estudio del Instituto de Karolinska de Estocolmo

INFIDELITY AND MACHISMO

In the era of Mexican golden cinema, the movies culturalized several generations, and influenced the daily lives of families, normalizing machismo and having a double standard; in most of the movies, the macho man who has a wife and many children predominates. The man, a green-tailed lover who was willing to conquer the young woman who would let herself fall in love, of course, for this he had to have money, land, etc.

The wealthy lords had children everywhere and everyone knew it and even applauded it, it was a pride to know that they were children of the philandering man. This was a trend in Mexican society and with the movies it became even more ingrained in society's beliefs.

The man in Mexican society was free, he was the head of the family and no one could question or judge him. The woman had no other life than to take care of the family and the home. She could not even think of setting limits or authority in her home, she would rather be considered a slave of the family and society.

She justifies herself in her mind and removes all guilt, she works so hard, "she has to give herself a treat." The wife waiting for a detail, always avoids his gaze and they wonder why he does not leave, because, although he does not admit it, you are the one who gives him peace and truth.

INFIDELITY BECOMES YOUR IDENTITY

The cheater always has an accomplice who challenges him to break the rules. The first step of the unfaithful is very difficult, then he becomes a conquering wolf, he likes the game so much so that he is looking for the next prey. Infidelity becomes his identity, it gives him a sense of belonging, he loves this way of life.

His principles are negotiable, depending on the occasion.

Being honest, being upright, comes second, yes, values are important in his life, but he has double standards, he will apply these principles when the occasion arises, he knows how to talk to women, he is a good actor during the relationship, his values are adjusted, depending on what the next partner has in his chest.

THE CHEATER AND HIS EXTRA EXPENSES

The cheater plays on two fronts, he wants to have his wife waiting for him with a warm meal, his children welcoming him with open arms, everything special. On the street he is free, he has a world at his feet, a variable schedule, one day he arrives late, the other earlier. The money he earns covers his needs and more, he can indulge himself, he is happy because life has been adapting to his expectations. He has a wife and a *girlfriend,* a complicated life, but it fills his senses.

These are some of the opinions *of girlfriends* who have dared to tell a little part of their story:

I am the girlfriend who nourishes his ego, I admire and love him, I fill him with affection, I make him feel special, it is not much work, it is one or two hours a day and when I can, it is a little more, that is why he gives me what I ask of him. I have a full tank of gas, he pays the rent, he buys me lunch, he feels dreamy because in the end he shows me off, everyone at work knows it and keeps quiet, they all play the same game, everything is normal....

We saw each other and we like each other, we are both married, and I have problems with my partner because he doesn't dedicate time to me, he doesn't care what I do as long as I don't bother him and follow my life.

He is a good match, he can pay me everything I ask for, he is very accommodating, and I like to feel cared for, he gives me what no one has given me and I feel special, he has become something important in my life and I don't want to lose him, feeling protected is the most primordial thing, we are planning to live together, this would be ideal and with time we are going to achieve it.

I live the way I want; I have one who pays my phone, another one pays my rent and utilities, I have five boyfriends. When I finish with one, or he leaves, I replace him with another, this is easy, it is an exchange of pleasure and they know it. If I work, I have my part-time. In this life you have to be abused and everything has a price, if they want, then let it cost them and let them pay.
It seems unbelievable, but it is the reality of many young women. They conquer whoever can pay for their needs. When they get bored or find someone else, nothing happens. It is the most normal thing, they go jumping from one to another, they consider it a way of life.

While I was in a meeting, a girl said to me:

-I'm trying to get pregnant and no matter how hard I try I can't, ¿what do I do? I tell her:

¿One more child? ¡you already have three! She continued, saying:

Yes, but I don't want my boyfriend to leave me, and I want to have a child with him. I looked at her astonished:

But your children are already grown up, you already have more freedom and with another child it is starting all over again.

Yes, but I want to tie this one up.

¿Why didn't you tie up the other children's parents?

I couldn't do it, because they were married …

I went out with a fireman and he gave me a schedule so I can call, I don't care, I talk to him at the time he tells me, for me it's a business, he gives me rules, I follow them.

One lady told me that for being with him once a week, he gives me two hundred dollars, and I already have that extra money for my expenses.

This is more common than you might think, I interviewed several people, and for them it is the most normal thing

A VOID THAT IS NEVER FILLED

When you are an expert conqueror, you get a quick conquest. A night of sex without condition. The pleasure is rich, but it only lasts a short time, in the end you are left alone with your loneliness, you become addicted to occasional pleasure without commitment. Nothing seems new to you, you don't care about anything, you are not moved by anything and an emptiness is created inside that nothing can fill.

You yearn to feel loved and appreciated, wanting is not love, everyone can love you because it is something superficial.

¡Love, such a rare thing!... Love fills, complements: it makes you see everything new; it makes you vibrate. It awakens in you the dormant joy and inspiration. Thus, the conqueror is like a whirlpool where the center is empty, and the surroundings sweep away everything in their path. Only loyal and unconditional love can fill this existing emptiness that is carried in the soul.

¿WHY DOES HE GET ANGRY WHEN HE GETS DUMPED?

You wake up to the harsh reality,
when the game you played
on two courts is over.
Now you can see your actions,
know that you lost a sincere affection,
a home with warmth,
when you arrived they were waiting for me with joy,
all that has changed, it's over,
I was no longer tolerated my condition of believing
I had the right to love outside the house
and arrive at the house to be attended to.
Your comfort is over.

"HAVING ARGUMENTS"

To make decisions you have to be well informed, exaggerated doubt, exaltation, worry and anguish is born in you, because you don't know what is happening to you, or you know it, but you don't assume it, and therefore you are not in control.

¿ Do you feel that what is happening to you makes no sense? analyze it and name it. ¿ Are you condemning yourself to a relationship of abuse? or ¿abandonment? ¡End this! ¿What resources do you have? ¿ don't you have money, and can't you get out of the relationship now? Start by making a life plan for yourself for the future.

First, save as much money as you can, look for all your exit doors from this relationship: prepare yourself physically, mentally, and emotionally for this important step that is the end of this relationship. Only when you externalize it, you see inside you and then you can act.

OVERPROTECTED BY A MACHO MAN

Culturally, women were raised to be overprotected by the man or partner. He provides comfort to the woman, even if she is independent. He knows how to cover her needs, emotional, physical, social, material, sexual; he does everything to know he is important and to be admired by his partner.

This is great, and it would be a perfect complement, if the woman did not have to put aside her world and lose her independence.

¡You lack nothing, I am your everything! - they often say. This can be a perfect plan of manipulation. The verb kills independence (verbo mata independencia) The home and the partner have to be the center of attention, absorbing all the woman's time completely and she has to put aside everything she has achieved.

Recently my friend Chris was talking to me. She was very devastated. She had realized that her husband had cheated on her. I asked her, how did you know? she told me: everyone knew, he posted some pictures on Facebook.

She was in a terrible crisis.

She told me.

- I already confronted him, and I asked him:

tell me, ¿where did I fail? I left everything for you, I was independent, I had my business and I left it because of your demands for attention, harassment and guilt that you make me feel! Always with your extra comments:

-No one does things like you do, you always know where everything is.

He was so insistent on me quitting my business, until he convinced me. At what point did I let myself be convinced, and؟ give myself up to satisfy you? And she continued telling me upset -

Now that he was unfaithful to me, I have nothing, now I have to work to get out of this situation and I have no experience in anything, the bank accounts and the money are his, everything is in his name, how is it that I allowed everything in his favor and let so many years go by? It's as if you were waking up from a nightmare! How hard it is to realize the reality!

FIXATIONS FOR JUSTIFICATION

Human beings generally justify their behavior when they want to cover up their mistakes. When a person likes the game that entertains him and gives him pleasure, he looks for all kinds of excuses to justify himself to others and to himself in order to continue with his eagerness and not feel guilty.

A few summers ago, we went on vacation with my family, and we agreed with some dear friends and their respective partners to come and visit us at the estancia where we were staying. The conversation was very pleasant, and we began to recount how many years we had been in our respective relationships. One of them, Tito, his name was, having more than a few drinks, said: "*Celia and I have been happily married for twenty years.*

We were all amazed and said: "Wow, that's smooth. To which he continued saying:

- Yes!!!, but with several girlfriends included, otherwise just imagine, what a stamina!

Tito continued talking without being too forward, because he felt confident, saying that he was proud because he looked for those distractions to be able to continue and endure the relationship. Of course, we all took it as a joke, including the wife....

This is learned conditioning; it becomes a justification that doesn't help anything in the relationship.

THE DECISION YOU MAKE IS THE KEY

Everything you say to him invalidates him, makes you feel that you are the one who is wrong and out of place, which causes you a state of anguish, sadness, and depression. You don't sleep, you are in a bad mood, the discomfort persists, you fight about everything, you don't like the things that used to make you happy, the relationship is poor, there is no more illusion, there is no more joy or trust, there are no more goals to achieve as a couple, much less communication, nor emotional connection. You feel weak, withered.

Your heart and soul are subjected to your sadness which generates other harmful emotions. So much abuse and denial of what is happening traps you more and more. At some point you must declare it's over! This must stop, because it is diminishing my personality and my joy.

"break the ropes, walk away and use your life as you wish."

"Don't stand in front of a light bulb, if the bulb burns out you will be left without light."

Don't let yourself be dominated by hate, it is a "poison", don't let fear dominate you because fear makes you act without sanity.

The decision you make is the key and you have to make it with great certainty. Don't let so much anguish, despair and disappointment affect your decision, you know that you have to act now.

YOU RESIST THE LOSS AND MAKE HIM COME BACK

To forget is what hurts the most when you are still hooked on that person. When you know you have lost him -because you can't have him anymore- and you want the attention again, you start thinking about what captivated you about his personality, you exalt all those qualities, details, and turn him into an ideal man.

You think about him, about his love for you, "*he was so special*", you say, you create a stronger attachment, which becomes obsession. You resist the loss and now you want to conquer him, whatever it takes, you become what he likes, you lose weight, you cut your

hair, you achieve your goal and "he comes back", and so does the usual.

The manhunter is finally back to his old ways and you know you have to go back to acting the way you did to win him back, it's a never-ending game.

Here you lose yourself by focusing on him, you make him more confident -him- about you, and you create a stronger ego than he already had; creating a perfect narcissist who thinks he is God on earth, that's how you make him feel. By concentrating on him, you have stopped being you, and your inner self asks you: ¿who am I? ¿Do you want me not to forget you?

Start with you, not to forget yourself, recover your values. What you were one day, and you left because it did not fit the marriage or his character, you put aside what you liked because there was no time and you had to leave your dreams.

Everyone was a priority but you. If instead of pleasing him, you please you, ¿what will you find inside you? ¿ Aren't you curious?

If you do a damage adjustment for all your losses - by focusing on him - you can reverse the roles, step back, focus on you with the same emphasis you put on him. Connect to yourself to grow and receive what is truly yours. You are going to become what you really are.

That person who now plays with your feelings, will see your change, because of his ego he will do everything possible to get you back, he will want to rescue what was lost, those details, that crazy personality that you laugh, dance, play, all those gifts that he took away from you... but you will be unattainable for him. Learn to laugh for yourself, make yourself a rich stew just for you, see how beautiful you are.

When he realizes that you no longer dedicate time and attention to him as before, that is when he will want to turn to see you, you will not pay attention to him. You will finally realize how blind you were, and you will enjoy the blessed freedom of being yourself.

Don't stand still, reveal yourself, he will have to respect your decision, your changes. You know he will not take his eyes off you, he knows you can captivate any man you want; you are empowered, he knows you are special, intelligent, seductive, original and you have the gifts to be whatever you want. *GOOD LUCK*

MACHISMO

In ancestral times we were led by the matriarchal power where the woman guided with peace and harmony. The man fulfilled his role as hunter and protector of the home, the woman took care of the family, sowed and guided the community wisely, so it was for a long time until the religious power wanted control for them and the only way was to subdue the woman, discrediting all her knowledge of wisdom making her weak and vulnerable because of the feelings of maternal love for the man.

"They said that a woman will never give up her husband and even less a child, that the woman is overcome by her feelings."

The woman was subdued by many religious and institutional interests, from minimizing her intelligence and humanity, to turning her into a thing, an object, they took away all her merit. To be able to do this they did it through the man who was given all the power over the woman, raising the patriarchy and phallic cult, changing at their convenience the religious and ancient beliefs about the value and quality of women.

[5]The social influence of machismo within the same families, were creating misogynistic, insensitive, irrational men who mistreat women and worst of all is the woman who encourages all this.

Infidelity is an emotional, social and spiritual mistreatment that directly affects women and their children. It is a behavior taught for the convenience of those in power.

---

[5] El origen histórico de la violencia contra las mujeres. Pilar Perez

FAMILY AND MACHISMO

Men have been conditioned through culture, social media and family pressure to respond to the demands of being a male. In the home, men and women are taught completely different behaviors, men are to be free and do what they want, and women are to be demure and ask for permission.

The submissive woman will be manipulated so that her goal is to get married and be dependent on her partner.

In the maternal home, many times the mother does not want to lose power and control over the son, making all kinds of tricks so that the son does not give himself fully to her relationship. Most couples have problems because the family does not allow the man to be noble and attentive to his partner, the mother feels betrayed and puts pressure so that the man does not have a good marital connection.

The mother-in-law uses the son as the executor of subjugation to bend the woman's character, and so that the daughter-in-law does not have what she never had. The mother executes her power through him.

They have created in the man beliefs that he is superior to the woman and puts her under his foot, he does not want to walk beside her, only in front of her, he doesn't know that his partner makes him strong, that she gives him the emotional balance he needs to survive in this complex life, full of confusion and contradictions. Family contamination has turned him into a puppet where he loses his soul.

In the society where we live, it is very common for women to be mistreated by a man influenced by his mother or sisters. Many times, I have seen how mothers-in-law subjected their daughters-in-law through their sons. They told them how they should treat them, and they imposed the limits and rules in the relationship.

THE MAN

Man is educated to be a protector, provider, and hunter.

Biologically, both men and women are formed through the fertilization of an egg by a sperm. The woman's egg with its progesterone hormone, and the man with his testosterone hormone makes possible the formation of the embryo, the union of the woman and the man, perfect combination.

The mother holds the child in her womb for nine months and it is a union of mother and child in all chemical, biological, and emotional aspects. The baby feels the emotions of its mother, who is emotional, sensitive, and protective. It also feels the male presence, strength, shelter and love of the father. The baby experiences the sensations and emotions of the mother and father and is an integral part of him, of his natural being that nurtures and integrates him as a living being.

From birth, the child has been marked and created a "denial" of what is his natural nature, of an emotional being. Most men have been educated to be providers, caregivers, they have been imposed a superiority over women that has severely damaged them because it is a denial to themselves.

Nobility, sensitivity to connect with his feelings and express what he feels; he has been created different from the woman, I have imposed an irrational comparison.

The woman is very capable and has created a weak image under the strong and tough man. The woman cries, the man cannot cry if he does, he's a sissy. The woman has to do the housework and the boy does nothing, because the woman is there to serve him. For the man, this is an emotional contradiction that leads him to an existential crisis because he never finds where to land his emotions and the unconditional love he feels in his heart cannot be expressed.

He loves in a very intense way and at the same time the woman he loves is inferior to him, creating an emotional void that he always tries to fill with an ideal woman that never arrives, because none of them is enough for the fictitious image that society has created for him. This is very dangerous, because I have seen many cases that end up in vices like alcohol, drugs, sexual addictions, irrational aggression etc. Even worse: suicide.

(movies: The Black Sheep, Sex, Shame and Tears, The Perez Family).

THE WOMAN

A woman's nature is one of freedom, she has the natural gift of wisdom and knowledge in her DNA; this genetic inheritance is transmitted to women through the female lineage, that is why women know everything, they intuit, smell, feel, perceive, sense, guess and it's true, when mom tells you something, pay attention and wait for results.

The woman has a deep connection with the earth, she has the biological capacities to create life. She has the extrasensory power that perceives energy and can read the environment around her, alerts her if she is in danger, has a broad vision of every situation she is living in and has the capacity for resolution and contemplation.

If the woman suspects something, it is because it is happening. So, learn to see your signals, hunches, perceptions, and you'll be right. When a woman loves, she gives her soul and knows how to love a real man.

Woman and man are perfect and are the center of creation on earth, there would be no humanity without this perfect union.

WOMAN, SEX SYMBOL

The media, movies, social media have worked to make sexuality the greatest pleasure for men. The man has to be an expert in the subject of love, to know how to exploit it with everything and everyone.

Most of the media expose women as a symbol of seduction, status and at the same time of submission. What a contradiction! The social system has used men to subjugate women in irrational complacencies. Everything has been corrupted and the woman has been subjected to the same social game for money or social convenience.

The role of woman and man to complement each other, to nurture and balance each other has become unbalanced. Men have been bombarded with seductive images where being faithful to a woman is the most boring thing. This takes him out of focus from harmony with his family, from the growth of a stable economy, from the education of his children, from a dignified retirement and a prosperous legacy.

The man doesn't know, he has not realized how much he needs his companion, her warmth and company, her endless talks, her wisdom, her guidance, her emotional support, because of so much external pressure he does not know how happy he is and the treasure he has from a woman who loves him unconditionally.

He loses his identity, his feelings of contradiction create an emptiness in his soul, creating an emotional imbalance that calms his senses with alcohol, cigarettes and the worst vices and diseases, until he ends his life early.

IS INFIDELITY A VICE?

Infidelity is the expensive and terrible vice that destroys everything around it. It is based on beliefs that are not based on reality, but what is reality, what I think, see, and hear?

It is pure confusion, a reality created by the society of lies, the family reinforces it, and the woman is the one who suffers it. This is very difficult to break, it is a vice of power, pleasure and emotion, these people only conquer, they fall in love with the infatuation and when that is over they lean towards someone else, they are afraid of true love, they see the superficial, they can have deep conversations and talk about the truth, but not his truth, he knows how to talk to the woman of sincerity, a sincerity that he does not know, he only imitates. Every day he feels emptier, he does not feel true or in fullness, everything tires, even the most pleasurable vice.

Even if he wants to, he cannot stop, because pleasure is one of the most difficult drugs to quit, it is an addiction supported by social and communication media where movies or series are broadcasted in children's time, which normalize inappropriate behaviors or modify the correct way of seeing the human sexual response, and of course, infidelity and sex move the money industry, buy the delight of pleasing; without money there is no pleasure.

To give up this vice, you must have a great loss and/or have fallen deeply in love and have a different level of consciousness, this will be a real challenge. Even if he is in love, he will not miss any pleasurable opportunity, it is a little adventure, nobody will notice it, but he will, in each little adventure he will reinforce his behavior because his brain, accustomed to pleasure, sees it as normal, it creates a co-dependent relationship in the woman of conquest, he gives her comforts to be indispensable for her, it is a way to trap the woman who has to be for him, she lives in enchantment, that is not love, it is an obsession and he becomes a slave of passion, where he feels that he is given life, but in reality he is killed, it is living in fantasy, every woman is an idealized creation for him.

When he gets tired of it, he withdraws without turning around, no matter the broken feelings of guilt, he just leaves, for him there is no perfect woman and if there were, he would ruin her. These people get hooked on emotion and it becomes a vice, every vice is expensive, fortunes are lost in them, like gambling addicts. His mission in life, if he knew it, he didn't want to work on it, he indulged his taste and emotional fantasy.

WHY THE UNFAITHFULL DOES NOT LEAVE?

He doesn't leave because home is his base of reality, so as not to feel lost, he arrives at a house where there is the warmth of home, where he enters a clean world, where there are no lies or betrayal. His betrayal weighs on him, but he makes up for it by saying "I have it good", he can't reproach me for anything, I fulfill the family.

He can deceive everyone, but he knows his truth. He doesn't leave the family for the sake of comfort.

BE ASSERTIVE WITH YOUR BODY LANGUAGE

When you have problems with your partner, the people around you can see it instantly, by your body language, your posture changes, your smile disappears, the anxiety shows in your eyes, in the restlessness of your hands, your way of speaking is altered. It is a sign of lack of self-confidence and self-empowerment.

The man knows you and knows that you are afraid, the fear you feel he can see in your eyes and in your tone of voice. Fear is one of the negative energies that blocks and does not let you see beyond. The brain reacts because it knows there is danger and your whole system is altered, you are in a constant state of alert, a reaction is triggered to fight or escape. If you are dominated by fear, you are in its hands.

Women are 100% driven by emotion and this can be a disadvantage or an advantage, it depends on whose hands you give yourself into. If he is an abuser, narcissistic, unfaithful and you show him your emotion, he will know very well how to manipulate you, dominate you so that you give him your will. But if he is a person who loves and values you, he will know how to support you at all times and be there for you, he would be a complement.

Thinking about this, analyze how since childhood you are taught to suffer for love, and it is reinforced in social media, movies, songs, etc. Suffering for love is a 100% profit making industry (heartbreak leaves money hand over fist for entrepreneurs, love is a round business).

Leaving high school, I saw a teenager who was behind her ex-boyfriend crying her eyes out, he saw her and ignored her, he continued walking, she noticed his attitude, but did not care and continued his stalking, I was on the same sidewalk, very close to her and did not give credit to the scene, it was very humiliating, I approached her and suggested that she follow me, but she did not accept, and continued behind him crying inconsolably, showing her suffering.

¿Where do you learn this? at home? ¿with your parents? I have asked myself a lot why we were educated in this way to humiliate us like this.

Love is not bargained for, it is given or not given, ¡period!

¿Why do you have to expose your vulnerability in such a way and let your innermost self be known? If you are in a vulnerable situation, it is better to cover all your feelings strategically, so you don't get more damaged than you already are.

I remember when there was a problem in my dating relationships and they would try to create a drama, I would say to them, "you want to end it?" They would say, yes or no, and I would make it easy for them, "well, you wanted to end it and that's it."

Sometimes remembering who you are, brings you more assertiveness than going around paying attention to other people's opinions or following patterns that are from people you respect, but in the end, it is them, not you.

You have to listen to your inner voice. Many times, I had already decided to end a relationship and when I asked for an opinion everyone told me: *"are you sure about what you are going to do? you are going to lose! remember that somehow you have a good husband and provider who loves your children.*" When you hear that, you freeze and leave your doubts behind and say, *"yes, that is right, I don't see the reality.* And you enter your comfort zone, you hold on tighter so that the doubt that is going around in your head doesn't show up anymore.

When you have problems with your partner, don't externalize it with your body language, because your state of mind can be seen and you show it to the one who has less to see it, even if you have the biggest problems in the world, keep your posture firm, your shoulders well squared and don't let the emotion overtake you. This will lead you to succeed in any situation, because when you have this attitude, the brain responds to not fall, and will give you more advantage that the other does not know that you are in their hands, it will serve to let the other know that you are firm and you can negotiate, set the rules and limits that you deem most appropriate.

THE ONE WHO GETS ANGRY LOSES

Don't get upset, stay calm, because when you lose control, you always want to win by arguing, imposing, blaming, and bending, and even if you win for well-founded reasons, in the end you lose the communication link in the personal, friendship or work relationship that you are interested in preserving.

It's a very fragile line, and you have to know how to keep it intact. Remember, maintain firmness, dignity, and cordiality, always keep your balance.

Sometimes, you have to be very astute, firm in your arguments. Don't give her the weapon of saying, ¡*I can't talk to you!* ¡*because you get upset about everything!"* and she confronts you in front of others so that you lose control and says, "*You see, that's why the relationship is over,*" she cancels you out and puts you in front of everyone as the hysterical crazy person who can't be talked to. Do not give him that weapon against you, always override you first with reason, that will give you calm.

THE DIGNITY OF WOMEN IN A FRACTURED HOME

Many people have gone through hell with a relationship that has fractured to the point that they have not been able to regain trust in the person. Something has been broken, which cannot be repaired, it is a very cruel reality.

You can't leave the house thinking only about yourself. Any sensible person is going to think: what is going to become of their children, and they know that they have to have a decent place to live with them. They stay in the marriage, but without having any intimate ties with their partners.

Some brief stories:

In a chance encounter in a supermarket, Celia comments to me: I can't do anything to change his infidelity, but I can have my dignity properly in place.

On another occasion, Teresa comments: He asked me to come back and forget the past. I replied, "*yes, because the past is yours, because if it were mine, ¿you wouldn't say the same thing, would you?"*

Many women, the way to regain their dignity, is to break the intimacy by sleeping apart.

Tere tells me determinedly: I have to endure more, my peace is the most valuable thing I have, and I do not have intimacy again.

THEY FAIL

They fail because they want to.

¿Why does the person we care most about betray us?

I was asking a friend, "*Why did he fail me, I don't understand.*" And she answered me: "*they failed me too.*"

They fail because they decided to, no one forces them, they feel sure of themselves, of what they gave one day for the relationship, until one day their promises lose their sweetness, strength, and emotion.

His lack of commitment fractured the relationship, it no longer made sense for him to stay here, they play superheroes having a double standard with a life of hidden pleasures that becomes pure adrenaline, that you can no longer calm down.

Because he is in a world of play and pleasure, lies and betrayal where one is left out of the emotional game, of the forbidden and unattainable, living on the sly running away from you, and you eager to regain home, ¡how ironic!

You are one more piece on his chessboard that makes it more exciting. He has learned to take care of you, he becomes an accomplice of everyone but you, you are the obstacle he has to overcome with the best strategy to be victorious.

His love is unattainable because you are in the way to achieve his fantasies.

WOMEN FORGIVE VERY QUICKLY

¡You always forgive him, so he won't leave! you want a good and you are doing yourself a wrong. Reinforce the behavior of the unfaithful where he knows that after a good meal he will return to the comfort of his home.

Know and feel indispensable and well received because he finally came to his senses and deserves the best, to be well cared for, so that he doesn't leave again, with the bad woman, easy woman (zorra).

He has returned and you received him with open arms, there was no regret or commitment to you, and he does not have to do it because that is what he has always done, and he is already used to it.

But this is not the man's fault, it is the woman's fault. The woman for not losing him spoils it, forgiveness without any consequence, on the contrary, he becomes more cynical every day, because of course if his behavior is rewarded and even more reinforced, he is like a capricious child that you buy all his whims, he makes all kinds of tantrums to manipulate you until he gets out of your hands and becomes "insolent."

There is never going to be a change if you forgive too quickly, don't give him time to come to his senses, he doesn't feel lost and doesn't value you. What you want to keep, one day you are going to lose because you have taught that man to be a cheater, a liar and unfaithful.

You have realized the deception and yet you receive it, *not even asking for forgiveness* (my friend told me) you reinforce his behavior, and you are part of that which you do not want to live. Forgiveness doesn't guarantee any change in their behavior when there are no consequences, that's why the individual is not corrected.

If on the other hand there is no commitment and value to the partner,

¿why should he change? He will only change until you hit bottom in not wanting to live this hell, while he lives in the glory of pleasure.

HITTING ROCK BOTTOM

If letting go will teach me to discover a new path, I am willing to change. Forgive myself, because I was an accomplice and allowed the abuse.

I thought that the other person had to change, because I was wrong, because he had to recognize our love! While I was thinking about this, I heard the voice of my sister, who once said to me: "*And why don't you change*?" ¿Me? ¿How can I change? "I'm perfect!" A long time passed, and her words echoed in my mind.

I realized that the one who had to hit rock bottom was me! It was a reality shock that shook me to the depths of my soul!!!!

"*Hitting rock bottom*" I felt emotionally stuck in the mud, and that I had been there for a long time, I knew I had to do my best to get out on my own, no one could get in for me, because they didn't know where I was, only me, I had to swim to get out and not turn around or stop because if I didn't sink and stay stuck in pain, bitterness, and disappointment, I couldn't sink and become impregnated with that.

I could not allow myself to be gloomy, bitter, envious,

and frustrated, I had a hard time overcoming my ego, accepting that I had to hit rock bottom, but this took a blindfold off my eyes that made me see a reality that I would never have thought I had. To know how to lose and let go, to let go, to have to heal and find a new horizon for myself.

I applied my own therapies. If they had worked for other people, they had to work for me. I had already taken the first step and it was the recognition of my mistake, to love someone who no longer belonged to me.

LIVING IN THE PAST, AVOIDED THE PAIN

The present was very painful, and I avoided it as much as I could. When I was asleep, I rested and escaped. It was better to live in the past, because there was still no pain or loss.

Living in the past you see life go by, you live with phantom memories that I longed for them to come back and be my reality again, no matter how hard I tried to relive the past, the memory was a memory and it screamed at me that it was no longer my reality.

Life goes on, it does not stop, when I realized that I was stuck in the past I stopped in my tracks and ran to my present, I saw myself alone with portraits full of memories in my hands that weighed a lot, the emotion weighs on the soul and you cannot carry it anymore, the weight of the memories pushed me back. To get out of that emotional state I had to let go little by little. I was releasing one by one those memories that one day were of passion, joy in my life and that I had to leave in the past.

I had to end cycles and I had to do it well, I did not want a stormy inner world so I embraced each memory and gave it its special place and I left them sheltered so they would not stick to me again. When there were only a few steps left to finish letting go of the past and reach my goal I felt light, I felt I wanted to fly, I no longer carried anything that weighed me down, when I crossed the threshold of the goal, I felt I was walking on a different path, everything seemed new, I saw beautiful things in life that I did not see before, they were everyday things, but now I look at them full of astonishment and surprise.

My new path began to be light, in this journey, I no longer wanted to carry anything or anyone.

ADDICTION TO NEGATIVE THOUGHTS AND EMOTIONS

I could not get out of so much anguish, until I made peace with myself and my former partner. I thought that was enough, but this was only a part of the whole. All that tremendous emotional burden, I can only compare it to a huge earthquake of 10.0 on the Richter scale, which had destroyed everything in its path.

But with this indulgence of forgiveness, I was able to bring a little peace to my heart, but the aftershocks of that tremor were still very much present. As the simple fact of hearing the phone ringing, upset me and my heart began to beat at full speed, my mind began to work at a thousand per hour, and more at lunchtime, I had tachycardia, because at that time he used to call me and ask me ¿*where are you*? and I would tell him " at home", then he would ask me to talk to someone in the family or ask me about someone, he would do this to make sure I was at home, he didn't want me to realize what he was doing at lunch time.

Anxiety and tachycardia tormented me at the same time, even if he didn't call me, my anxiety was triggered when I knew he was leaving work, the smells of perfumes irritated me and made me angry, ¡because he always arrived smelling like a woman's perfume! For me it was a torment and so many other situations that triggered my emotions. I knew that this had to stop or at least control it. It was a very traumatic experience. I already had a biological clock of emotional disturbance that embraced me and no matter how much I wanted to avoid it, it would go off.

I realized that I had become addicted to the chemistry of emotions and negative thoughts, and that my body at a certain time was ready to feel and activate, at first, I generated them with anxiety and anguish that caused me what I was living, when I was already very affected by the situation, I wanted to avoid it, but it was activated automatically.

When I put up more resistance, a wave of emotions came to me, and although I wanted to stop them, they came to me from all sides, activating my emotion; it was a struggle that took time. When I was able to control the emotion of the relationship, the brain was already addicted to the anguish and adrenaline of negative thoughts and emotions, the brain now created uncomfortable situations that had not happened, but that I imagined as if they were true and activated a response of emotion that I wanted to avoid.

I took therapy and it was very helpful. I practiced a technique I invented. I drew an imaginary line, on one side was the past and on the other the present and crossing from the past to the present, I was forbidden to go to past emotions or memories that hurt me. I had had enough.

TAKE AWAY YOUR ATTENTION

If someone hurts you, take away the most important thing you have, which is your attention. Well, everything you focus on grows, envelops you and you become part of it, whatever it is.

It was not easy to reach this decision, I had so many emotions that I was suffocating, it caused me anxiety attacks, it is as if the emotion swallowed you and exploded inside, I could not take it anymore, I said, enough is enough! This must stop and the only way I found to stop it was letting go. Letting go, because you get to the point where you lose and, in the end, it is a power struggle with yourself.

I only thought of the betrayal, the tyranny of his attitude towards me, he came only to see what he asked to get out of here, he seemed like a ¡bird of prey! just looking, and at the precise moment he snatched and saw him and had a lot of distrust, worst of all is that it had a double face, and it confused me

At a certain point, I came to think that the crazy one was me.

I was confused because he had always been affectionate at a certain point, I came to think that I was the crazy one.

There were terrible emotional fights that threw me to the ground, and I had to let go of the emotion and be smarter and know how to fight with a manipulator.

At the beginning I could not accept that this person, who was in front of me, had been the same person with whom I married one day I was very much in love, I felt an unbearable pain in my soul, my heart hurt me, the loss of a love that was so beautiful and now that same person was the one who hurt me the most, that upset me a lot, it hit me with everything, I had a lot of anger, resentment, anger, tension, sadness, anguish and pain.

I felt that at any moment I would lose my mind, that I would fall into madness and lose control, it was a bomb that would explode at any moment and there was only a small and fragile line between madness and mental stability. So much thinking, turning over the same idea and turning it over for hours and hours, thinking until I was exhausted.

There were even times when I could see myself running away, screaming, pulling my hair, I got scared and it came to my mind, a friend of mine who ended up in a psychiatric hospital had such a strong nervous breakdown, that she was blocked, as if she was lost, she didn't respond to anyone and she stayed like that for a long time.

I could not expose myself and lose myself, I had to have control because there was so much at stake! I was only seeing the pain of the loss, and not the legal part. I had to put my feet on the ground, for me and for my children, because if I did not fight, who was going to do it?

My children's attitude hurt me to my soul, but I could not speak bad of their father, although I was very angry, I did not want to put them in the middle of a fight, besides he was using and manipulating them, and one day they had to realize it for themselves because the truth always comes to light and I had to be wiser to protect them, so I was kind to them and to everyone, I already had a decision and a plan, and whatever their attitude was, I just had to follow my plan, I no longer put emotion into anything that could confuse me, I took my attention away from the situation, I just acted to get the results I wanted.

He, whatever he did, or tell my children what he told them, I always thought he acted well, so that they had no excuses to blame me. One of many days I was in the car waiting and I wanted to listen to music, I did not bring my glasses and I pressed without seeing the next song and a message came out: ***Let yourself be guided, you are not alone, who bothers you so much, take your attention away***. I felt a lot of peace after that, I always received random messages, which calmed me down and I no longer felt alone, a wonderful power was with me, I could feel it.

YOU STOPPED ME WHEN YOU SAW ME GO

You didn't love me anymore,
you forgot my love,
the value I gave to your life
and how strong we were together.

You were so sure of me
that you didn't realize
how I was fading from your life.

When you lost me,
you wanted to hook me with our memories
and that worked for you,
but the memory lost more meaning
and value every day

and the day
came when they stopped mattering
and it didn't work for you anymore.

When you see me ready and determined?
to leave with many plans,
then you get scared that I will leave you,
you change your mind
and now I do suit you,
you want to enter my life and my world again,
trying to stop me from leaving.
I already stopped myself many times,

and in the end, it's the same thing.
I have already played your game many times
and your change of attitude

begins to make me believe
that you are the special prize,
the splendid one,
the attentive, affectionate, the protector!

You are a character out of series,
now I can see it,
"The one who can do it all",
but in the end, you were a wolf
who let himself be hunted,
before I was inside your reality!
I lived between reality,
lies and my hallucination,
I could no longer find myself,
I lived between memories,
disappointments and lies
and a little bit of reality.
Each act of yours was gradually fading my illusion,
my pleasant memories no longer weighed so much,
weighed more the desire to leave you
and create a new reality.

I FORGAVE MYSELF AND RESTORED MY JOY

I had already let go and forgave myself, but I could not find my joy. It was as if many negative experiences had erased it in me, ¡I wanted to laugh and I did not know how!

I had to remember a pleasant experience; I remembered my adolescence in high school where I was very happy. I didn't know love yet, joy was mine (I didn't depend on anyone) clean and pure. Simple and easy things made me happy, playing basketball, walking in the rain, dancing in the streets. I will use my joy to recognize and restore myself.

I would ask people who had appointments with me (as a hypnotherapist), *"If you had a new opportunity to change your life, without setting any limits, how would you reinvent it?"*

You have the freedom to create a new world, you have you and what are you going to give yourself, ¿what do you expect from yourself?

God gives you a new beginning. When I remembered all this, I saw myself differently, I got excited, I felt my being beat for the first time in a long time, it came to my mind that young girl full of life with so many illusions walking in the University wanting to conquer the world.

It gave me a lot of hope and illusion to start a new world. I cannot turn back time, but I can create wonders with what I have at hand and that is me. If by forgiving myself I recover all of me, I will let go, with all that I have to let go and forgive, so that all that I am can return to me.

WE DO NOT RECOGNIZE LOVE

When we have love, we do not know how to appreciate it, we do not know how to receive it, or give it to the right person, we do not enjoy a relationship or feel gratitude for what we have. There is no satiety because of the emptiness that is carried in the spirit, and by not filling that emptiness, it is reflected in deep sadness of the soul, which makes us not appreciate a relationship when we have it.

¿What is it that confuses people? they go looking and looking for love, and when they find it, they play with it, break hearts and go to another relationship. Lucky is the one who, without searching, finds true love, it is like winning the lottery, but even so, people who win the lottery lose it, because they don't know how to recognize and appreciate it, that's why they lose the great love of their lives.

The media create a lot of confusion, on the one hand, they sell you pure and sincere love and on the other hand they also sell sexuality, which awaken a sexual desire without control, they incline you to be a hunter and not let go of any opportunity.

There are many temptations that confuse, not distinguish the desire with true feelings of love, and not to make mistakes, you have to analyze very well and be alert to life situations.

NO ONE IS GOING TO SOLVE MY LIFE

I don't wait for someone to come and solve my life, I must and I want to solve it myself, there is no one more powerful than oneself. When you trust yourself, when you are firm in your convictions, your beliefs, values and principles, this supports you in making the decision to end a marriage.

I read a lot about this subject, I wanted to be well informed about it and be one hundred percent sure of how I had to do the paperwork! I did not want to do things wrong and have the excuse that I did not know, I did not want to have the blindness of ignorance, so I had to do my homework well! Because, just as I received correct information that empathized with me, there was also distorted information and opinions that I could not have accepted at all. This was one of the reasons that motivated me to take professional therapy. Not only with one therapist, I consulted with several therapists and compared what each one said and if the information was repeated, I confirmed that he was right, and reaffirmed it with other sources. I did this on a personal and legal level.

PEOPLE'S OPINIONS

They told me. ¡Don't get divorced! All men cheat, at least you know this one and he gives you what you need. Let him live in the same house and have one room and you another, as if nothing had happened."

¡I could not! He asked me for a divorce, and I accepted it, but after a while he started to change his mind. If I had wanted to, I would have returned to the relationship, but I did not accept it, it was not the life I wanted. I felt overwhelmed and humiliated.

Suddenly, he came repentant, he thought that I was going to forgive him, no, I wanted to get out of this situation that has lasted too long

The disappointment and disillusionment were already stronger than the love I might have felt for him one day, and I was not going to stop and corner myself out of fear, I had already been imprisoned for a long time. They told me, "*you don't know what you are going to face! a divorce is very difficult*", ¡and I knew it!, but I didn't want to be imprisoned by my fears, I wanted to see beyond fear, I was always in the shadow of someone, first it was my family. My dad was very strict and then I got married and I was in a relationship where I was always a housewife, doing everything for everyone, and now I wanted to do something for me and by me.

They told me, "don't get divorced and have a person on the sly." What? No, not that, I can't imagine having a person on the sly. To do that, the person has to be married and I was not willing to play such a dirty game, like the one they played on me, and besides, seeing me in hiding is the same as being imprisoned. Living a lie, no, I am not looking for anyone, but if I were looking for someone, it would not be like that.

I understand that appearance and comfort is something very important for women, the fear of being singled out and feeling safe, and this is very understandable, and I respect it, but for me, to go back in there, was to return to madness, to the madness of not being me, for being in someone's shadow.

I love freedom, I have always loved it, being free has to be something beautiful, wonderful. We are all born free, alone and even if we are accompanied, we are the center of our own universe and we were not born attached to anyone, we were born alone, and alone we are going to die, and it is not to be scary, it is to adjust to reality.

I did not want to confuse myself more than I already was with ideas that fluttered in my mind, and this made me think about withdrawing from everyone, I wanted to be alone and find myself, to analyze what I had to do.

FORGIVENESS ARISES

I had a lot of pain, anger, resentment and anxiety from the loss. It was torture, my mind was spinning day by day and instead of diminishing, it was growing. I felt it stronger and worse, I wanted to have the power to punish that person and hurt him, to make him feel some of my pain, I wanted the attention I once had from him, but now, to make him feel my contempt, to give him where it hurt the most, I wanted him to pay me back for all those nights of pain that I cried myself to sleep.

I felt so lonely, and he looked so full, so happy and in love, it seemed that he was even floating, that filled me with fury; my mother commented *"don't suffer, he's enjoying, and you are suffering.*" They told me, "you have to forgive to free yourself from pain." It is difficult to forgive when you are struggling, you are on the defensive with grief on the surface; it was an emotional crossroads, I had to leave it to time, I had to let things flow because for the moment I could not forgive.

I wanted to get even, I knew I had to forgive, but I was not ready for forgiveness, ¿ how could I give it to him, if he had not even asked me for it? ¡That made me even angrier! ¡I imagined that he was asking for forgiveness and I was sending him to hell! That he was begging me, and I didn't listen to him; I enjoyed that feeling. Time went by and the destructive emotion was a vice, and every vice causes an emptiness in the soul, it was draining me, emptying me. If I kept it up, I was going to be stuck in frustration and I didn't want to look like all those bitter, sad divorced ladies.

I was not ready for forgiveness yet, but I knew I had to stop the adrenaline that was trying to explode out of me, it was like a car going a hundred miles an hour, and it was going to crash into a wall, I was afraid for my physical and mental health, so much anger, so much rage, ¡I felt like I was drowning! I thought, with this anxiety I could trigger a stroke to myself ¡I'm going to be all crooked!

This made me reflect. I was destroying myself. If forgiving that person was going to give me the peace, I needed so much and free me from so much anguish and anxiety, I am going to do it for me. I could not live in that hell of resentment; the damage was already done. I constantly asked myself, ¿why did he do it? ¿why me? ¡if I gave him the best of me! ¡You want answers to absurd questions! He always did what he wanted, without giving an explanation, ¡*you want to hear something that would convince you and/or give peace*! but you never be happy or satisfied with what he could tell you!

The answer was in me and I had to answer it, not him, I had to solve my emotional dilemma. Everything was already given, as the proverb says: "a stick is given and God doesn't take it away", I had to let go.

My children were with me and they were always watching, and they were anguished to see me with a lot of tension, and my main priority is that they were well and that they came out of this situation as little damaged as possible

It was not necessary for him to come to kneel down and ask for forgiveness, or to recognize all the damage he had done to me by his abandonment, he simply left, and I stayed here waiting, that's how I decided, he stopped loving me and I longed for him to love me. But the day came, I pulled him out from the center of my soul, from my heart, from my innermost being, because that was where I had him stuck and I pulled him out by the roots.

When I really had the firm conviction to let go and accept its absence forever, there was no turning back. I felt my freedom, as if some very heavy chains that I had carried for years had been removed, and the worst thing is that I did not feel their weight, I got used to carrying them, I felt so light that I could not understand it, I had an inexplicable relief.

It still did not justify the way the relationship ended in such a cruel way, but I decided not to be the judge and executioner, I felt that something was detached from me, it came out, it flew and instead of feeling sad, I was flooded with peace in my heart, in my soul and spirit. I let go, and if that is forgiveness, then I forgive him.

KNOW HOW TO WAIT TO PROCESS THE DIVORCE

"When divorce is imminent, you must evaluate and make movements at the right time at the convenience of the family members".

Although the situation was tense in the relationship in recent times, I thought about not being carried away by emotion and that it was convenient.

Negotiation, calm cordiality, and good treatment between the couple who, although they are no longer together, must prevail to reach agreements for the well-being of the whole family.

If you must wait for a medical treatment, a graduation of one of the children, a process of important papers, it is better to negotiate it and be on good terms.

If there are children in the relationship, they will always be a priority. Well, if this process is not handled properly, collateral damage will be impacted on the children, leaving them with a lot of pain.

I WAS SABOTAGING MYSELF

¡I idealized you!

Even when I had already lost you, we had already talked about the divorce and we agreed on many things, suddenly, a feeling of longing came over me, of nostalgia for what could have been and wasn't. This made me feel horrible, and every time I had to go through the divorce, I put it off again and again. This made me feel horrible, and every time I had to file for divorce, I put it off again and again.

When I walked to court, I felt like a zombie, I didn't want to face the pain, I didn't want to feel anything, I knew I had to do it, and days would go by, and something would come over me, and instead of feeling frustration, I would feel relief, I would say *"I haven't taken that step yet"*, and so time would go by. Until I realized that I alone was sabotaging the process so as not to face the grief.

I faced the harsh reality, I thought why delay all this? Even when he is home, sitting on the couch, his mind is somewhere else with someone else, absent and present, what irony. He still pouts, he just sighs and sighs that he is not happy! So, I went to court and didn't stop for a moment, until I finished the paperwork... ¡It's done! ... When I submitted the papers, I told him, *"go, go where you will be happy, and take your bitterness with you, you are infecting the whole family, having you here is the worst."* By not letting go, by postponing the mourning, the agony becomes more unbearable, and you get more damaged.

RESISTANCE

When making important decisions that transcend in our lives, we encounter resistance, and many times fear intervenes, obstructing, almost forcing you to let go. Resistance always appears to see if you can overcome obstacles, it is a test of the universe that challenges you to prove how much you want your goal. You only fight for the most precious thing and, when you achieve it, it tastes like glory.

Do not give up, do not let indecision dominate you. Don't let your goals get stuck because of insecurity and fear. Never abandon the projects you have dreamed of and idealized because it makes you become apathetic, critical, mediocre, lifeless and tasteless.

THE LAWYERS WERE TELLING ME, JUST GO AGGRESSIVE.

I consulted with several lawyers and most of them told me: "*go aggressive, let him pay your lawyer's fees.*" I think you can't assault and challenge someone because you bring out the worst in that person. It is a philosophy of mine, and for that you should not act aggressively.

Yes, I felt anger, rage. I was thinking in my mind "*until you destroyed everything, you realized what you had lost" but you reacted too late*!!! there is no coming back!!! it's over!!!!!

I had to overcome my courage, control it to the maximum, I felt like it was like a beast that was controlling all the time, and it was ready to go out and smash everything in its path without caring about anything. Although I was apparently calm, inside I was super aggressive, I had to dominate and keep calm with intelligence and cunning because there were people who wanted this to end badly, very badly, almost in disgrace and I was not going to allow it.

If this ends in a lawsuit, I would not be able to negotiate and I would lose more by giving free rein to my fury, no one will make me lose my sanity, it was my game and I had to win it, just as I had planned. Lawyers have their strategies, and I could not follow them because they went against mine.

He had his game too; he was always looking to upset me and create drama. A lawyer explained to me to be careful, because if *"you explode it could cause a lawsuit"*, they can declare you incompetent for custody of your son and put a restraining order or accuse me of domestic violence. After so much fighting I was not going to create yet another conflict, I had to know how to plan every fight I faced, I was exhausted from so much stress and many battles.

I became more assertive and carefully selected the battles I could fight. Several fights I let go without confrontation and they resolved themselves.

Who would have thought that the person I loved so much, the one who knows me best, who knows my vulnerability spots, knows where to hurt me, now is on the opposite side, as an enemy. This was the greatest lesson of my life.

THE DIVORCE

I had always believed in marriage, and by irony of fate, I was now going through my divorce. Everything had already been said. Things were going from bad to worse, there was no solution, I was so disappointed that I couldn't take it anymore and I let go, or ¡rather the marriage let me go!

One day I found a phrase that touched my heart: *"This is the answer to your prayers*", when I read it, I kept thinking and said, "*yes, I think so*." Although I longed for the marriage to be saved, that both of us could come to an agreement, but that evidently did not happen.

I firmly believe that God took pity and took it away from me. I heard one person say: *God already gave you the opportunity to leave him on your own and by your own means and you didn't do it, so hold on! because when God takes him away from you "you will know what pain is"* (AA) ...and then I believed it.

Out of nowhere I heard another phrase:
"When things are falling apart, it's because they are falling into place." I was tired, I had no more strength to fight, and I let go, I simply let what had to happen, and if it fell apart, it was time for me to see what I had been holding on to fall.

I did my homework, I researched everything that a divorce entailed, I consulted with several lawyers about my rights and explained my situation, I had to know the rules of the game very well and I had to play it better than anyone else.

I had given my life to my family and destiny had turned the game upside down, reality knocked at my door, that is why it was very important for me to know how I was going to solve my divorce, because I had to start from there for the future.

"Some women don't think about the future ... until the future comes too soon and catches you off guard."

He would see me coming and going from court and I would see him grieving, he would ask me, "*how*

did it go, did you do it yet?" In his eyes I saw regret and his expression told me to stop. His attitude was no longer challenging. Now he looked subtle, and kind, as if to persuade me not to do it. I could tell he didn't know how to act.
After a while, I finished the paperwork and "I got up the courage" (reyli song) and submitted the document to the court. I knew that the sheriff was going to arrive to deliver the divorce papers to the house and I set the earliest time they could deliver the paperwork.

I knew that, at that time, he was going to be at the house, and he had to receive it and sign it, a policewoman arrived, and he opened the door. I saw on his face the expression of anguish and he asked me with astonishment, "

¿*Why did you do it*?" "¿I did what?" I answered him, "¿The divorce paperwork?", I was puzzled, and I told him, "*Whaaat... ¡ I don't understand! you were always asking me for a divorce, you wanted to be free, ¡ well go now! there you have your divorce, you didn't tell me, ¡let me go! ¡please let me go! ¡so go! it was what you wanted so much¡ you got it! be happy, you fought so hard for your freedom ¡here it is!" "ask and it will be given to you" -bible. "¡No!" he answered me.... "I wanted you to show me to see what you wanted to ask for and to see how we are going to do it." I told him, "well", here are your papers that you asked for so much, and if you want to know how we are going to do it, read them and see how you are going to do it.*

The police were still at the door and saw him so lost that she told him, *"you have thirty days to answer."*

He had already seen several lawyers and they charged him more than me, for the paperwork and for appearing in court for $400 an hour. He was desperate. I asked him for what I was entitled to by law.

DIVORCE PROCESS

I researched what was involved in the divorce process, rights and laws. Generally, when I start a project, I put a lot of interest in it, especially this one, because it was obviously very personal. I did a complete search, but in this very personal and important situation I focused on everything. I knew I had to find a lawyer and I wanted to know the questions I had to ask, I asked people who had been divorced, I asked them for their lawyers' phone numbers.

All the information they give me I would write it down in my notebooks, and I would corroborate it again with someone else. I would get many different answers, so if I had a doubt, I would research it until I got a satisfactory answer.

Don´t go, only for what you want to hear, and sign a divorce contract.

They explained me how the process is going to be and how much cost.

They asked me for half of the process to stay as a deposit.

He had to pay for the divorce process, but the lawyer asked me for the advance to start the process (and fill out an extra form from the court where he said he would take care of the divorce expenses, then they reimburse the money until the process is finished and collect the money from him), it took two thousand to fill out all the forms, and from there, four hundred an hour. This was a contract, and if it got difficult divorce, you had to make a bond of some property or something of value that could pay the legal fees.

I called a friend and told her about my situation. I already had a lawyer chosen to represent me, but she told me to go to the court and that they had a (self-help) center where they would help you do your paperwork on your own.

I didn't want to do the paperwork myself, but the attitude of all the lawyers gave me a bad feeling. I felt like I was going to fall into a trap, and I didn't want to be stuck in a legal situation that would last for years. I looked for the information from the place my friend had told me about, because in the end I had all the documents they requested, I already knew what the divorce process was about, we had already talked about it and negotiated.

He had also asked several lawyers and they asked him for more money than they asked me, they also told him to be aggressive. He always asked me, "well tell me, what are you going to ask for", I answered him, *"what the law grants and you know very well what I mean", I told him, "you have already seen several lawyers and you know that it is going to be expensive, we better agree to solve this, without losing more than what we have already lost*"; by this point we were already very emotionally worn out and the best thing was to do our part, because if not, the only ones benefiting were the lawyers.

I went to court, and you must be one of the first ten people to be served. I organized all the papers I could possibly need, and I left very early. At the court there is an "self-help" department. They gave me three packets of forms that had to be filled out, I saw a lot of papers and I didn't know where to start. I read them and read them, I turned them over and organized them, there was a resistance in me that I couldn't explain. Anxiety, fear, sadness, I don't know. It was a strange feeling that I never would have imagined I would have to face.

I finally got up the courage and started to work on analyzing and filling out. I worked on the draft at the same time I was negotiating with him, I would go to court and the people from the center would see me arrive, they already knew they would have to make one more change, sometimes they would look angry, but I didn't mind, that was their job and they had to do it right. I always made sure there were no mistakes, I put a lot of time into it, but it would save me headaches, extra time and money that I didn't want to spend in the future.

Once I said to a guy who helped me at the help center, "for you it's just another day of work, but for me doing this legal paperwork is a personal challenge and I have to make it perfect." I took the time I needed to get it the way I wanted it, right, perfect.

The last day I had filled out all the forms, I was about to submit it and I said no, I will wait, I must review everything very well. I know that those who helped me were tired of me, but in me, there was a satisfaction that I cannot explain. It was the end of a cycle in my life. A new beginning where I achieved what I set out to do.

When the papers were complete, I submitted them to the court for a little less than five hundred dollars. I paid for the sheriff to deliver the paperwork, there in the same building is the office where they send the paper notice of divorce. He only had thirty days to respond to the divorce complaint, when he saw the paperwork, it was a little different from what we had talked about, but everything was fine (but if he agrees with what you filled out, and doesn't answer the paperwork, it goes on).

The court sent us to mediation. At the help center they gave me a phone number for Loyola University, which is a school for lawyers. The state provides funding for them to provide free professional mediation services, and to keep these cases from going to court and overcrowding the court. I called and they gave me an appointment, explained what it was all about and we decided to do the mediations with them.

At the end of the mediations, they filled out all the paperwork to submit to the court, so, after the process with them, they gave me the contract that we had signed, and I just went and submitted it to the court. I had to wait for the judge's approval (a stamped paper). When the paper arrived, I was happy because I had finally finished an overly complicated process that came out very cheap thanks to my astuteness.

WHAT YOU START WITH LOVE, FINISH WITH LOVE

There are couples that end in divorce because one of them starts fighting, lying, omitting and provokes a crisis to justify the separation, does not have the courage to accept that he/she is no longer satisfied with the relationship and provokes a hell for both, until the other one can't take it anymore and ends up asking for a divorce.

The couple ends up hating each other, "*all this is unnecessary, because if you really want separation, you can get it without creating so much chaos.*"

If you really want the separation, you can do it with the truth in front of you and without causing harm, this speaks a lot about the education and feelings of each person, that's when you realize who you really married, shows his true self.

Even to end a relationship, you must end it with dignity. There's an actor by the name of Roberto Palazuelos that got divorced and he said: "*what you start with love you have to end it with love*" it was a shock, I thought about it, I analyzed it, it was hard for me to digest it and I said... that is how ¡ I want to do it! I had to set a guideline, I had to have a plan of how I wanted to end my divorce.

I knew that this was going to define the future relationship between the two of us and with the others.

I FACED MY FEAR

When I was going through the divorce process, many times I was paralyzed by fear and I wanted to stop everything and reconcile. I drew strength from deep inside me and faced the fear. I was in a lot of pain from all that was involved in the situation, but in the end, I felt relief. When you look through fear, you fear losing, because you are insecure, you feel lost and because you are afraid of not losing, you lose more.

You see the fear, you observe it, you feel it, you palpate it, and you realize that you learned it as a child, it was always there, hidden. When I tried something new, it woke up, but I still challenged it and overcame it, accomplishing my goals. Now I know, after suffering so much from fear, now let fear be afraid of me!

Crossing the penumbra of fear, you find the achievements you fought for and the satisfaction brings you happiness.

DIVORCE PROCEEDINGS

Even if you hire a lawyer to initiate the divorce proceedings, you should be very well informed of what your lawyer is processing, so that you do not get unpleasant surprises where you are involved in complications that then trap you in a long process and you spend years without resolving your situation.

Be fair and rational in your request, As far as possible, be fair and rational in your requests, excessive ambition is useless, and make sure that the lawyer understands your requests. because among lawyers they know each other, and they put together their strategy. Don´t get trapped where you and your partner get into a legal battle spending money to defend each other.

The minimum they charge for appearing in a California state court is four hundred dollars per hour.

My friend Teresa had already paid about thirty-five thousand dollars for her divorce, and she still did not have a final decision, she was in limbo, nothing was resolved, it was one court after another, and the lawyer wanted more money.

Teresa did not want to give him anymore, and the lawyer said: "*Then you do it*". She has been several years into her divorce process, she is desperate! She is living a real nightmare, which, besides affecting her emotionally, she loses money every time she goes to court.

The saddest thing is that while the process lasts -and it has been going on for more than four years now-, she cannot go to her country because she does not want to leave her daughter.

The ex-husband does not want to let her go with her, he has to sign a travel authorization form and without that permission it is not possible for her to leave the country.

If someone is going to fill out the paperwork for you, make sure it is done correctly. Personally, I invested time in informing myself about this, to find out what I should do, what my rights were as a spouse under the law.

Invest time, get informed, because you must know what you are going to get into, you must know everything that a divorce implies, if not, in the long run it will be awfully expensive and complicated, and you will not be satisfied.

I always end up doing my own things, I like things to go as I plan them, even if I invest time. It is worth it; in six months it was all finished for less than five hundred dollars.

I am not a divorce lawyer who can give you legal advice, but I will give you a reference where you can look for information. Remember, look for accurate information and rely on someone professional as a divorce lawyer.

Make sure you know which court in the United States corresponds to you.
www.courts.ca.gov
www.lacourt.org/selfhelp
(213)830 0845
HELP CENTER THEY HELP FILL OUT THE PAPERWORK 8:00 A.M. 12:30 P.M
COURT SERVICE-COUNTY OF LOS ANGELES
LOYOLA LAW SCHOOL / LOS ANGELES MEDIATION CENTER www.lls.edu/ccr

PLAINTIFF
FORMS / FORMS TO FILL OUT AND SUBMIT IN ENGLISH COURT ARE ALSO AVAILABLE IN SPANISH.

FL-120 1 of 3 RESPOND-MARRIAGE/DOMESTIC PARTNERSHIP are 3 pages long.

FL-311 1 of 2 CHILD CUSTODY AND VISITATION are 2 pages long.

FL-341 (D) 1 of 2 ADDITIONAL PROVISIONS are 2 pages long.

FL-105/GC-120 DECLARATION UNDER UNIFORM CHILD CUSTODY JURISDICTION AND ENFORCEMENT ACT (UCCJEA) 1 of 2 are two pages

FL-150 INCOME AND EXPENSE DECLARATION 1 of 4 are 4 pages

FL-160 PROPERTY DECLARATION 1 of 4 are 4 double pages.

If the respondent agrees to everything you filled out on the forms and does not respond, continue the process, but if you do not agree, you have thirty days to respond and submit your packet with other forms.

RESPONDENT FORMS

FL-120 1 of 3 RESPONSE-MARRIAGE/DOMESTIC PARTNERSHIP

FL-311 1 of 2 CHILD CUSTODY AND VISITATION (PARENTING TIME)

FL-341(D) 1 of 2 ADDITIONAL PROVISIONS-PHYSICAL CUSTODY ATTACHMENT

FL-105/GC-120 1of 2 DECLARATION UNDER UNIFORM CHILD CUSTODY JURISDICTION AND ENFORCEMENT ACT (UCCJEA)

F-150 1 of 4 INCOME AND EXPENSE DECLARATION

FL-160 PROPERTY DECLARATION 1 0f 4 PROPERTY DECLARATION.

To fill out the forms, have all your documents ready to take the information. Bank accounts, savings accounts, car registrations, 401k stocks that some companies give to their employees (do your research), property titles, jewelry, furniture, etc.

You must pay a small amount of money to have the court notice delivered to your home, do not compromise any of your family or friends, it is better to pay to avoid misunderstandings and headaches.

HOW I MANAGED TOLERANCE TO REACH MY GOAL

To manage tolerance, I became an expert in observing each emotion, separating frustration from feelings, and analyzing them separately.

Tolerance is resisting before all kinds of tests, seeing beyond pain, having sanity to reach your goal. To is learning, facing, understanding and transforming emotion into something positive and applying it at the right time. It is giving time to each situation with patience, faith, and courage that everything will turn out well and to smile again.

He affirms every day:

"I will dedicate myself and focus on growing and developing a project, until I see results. With effort and will, everything can be achieved."

I GAVE MY ALL, UNTIL THE LAST CHANCE

I did everything to save my marriage and now I leave with no regrets. I leave with my head held high. I gave everything I had to give and every opportunity.

From this determination, no one will convince me to change my mind, nor will I waver from my decision; from now on, I am in charge of my life, I am not interested in social judgment or what they think of me.

MODIFY

Every time I thought of something, I analyzed it and modified it so that it would not cause me anguish, especially to my children. I was very attentive and careful not to fall into the emotion that was related to him, I didn't want any situation to alter my senses, what I heard and saw of him was no longer of my personal interest, that's why I got divorced, to let go of the situations that I didn't want in my life anymore.

Many people would call me to ask me how I felt or why I was divorced, to those I had to explain I would give them the basic information out of politeness and because we were close, I wanted them to know that I was already divorced.

They asked me if my ex was seeing anyone. I answered, *"I don't know, I've never asked him, or I haven't seen him.*" They would ask me, "*How are you feeling*?" I would tell them very well and they didn't expect this answer. "*And how are your children*?" and I would tell them well, very well, ¡they were surprised!

¡ There is no more anguish of a child than to see the mother anguished or afraid...! I was careful with my words and actions, not to talk about what had already happened and solved, I realized that every emotion has its chemistry and every time you tell you attract it back to yourself with strength and the same effect. When I got involved or fell with someone talking about how unhappy I was, I would feel anguish, despair and I would have a bad time that day, or even for a week.

Thought has its own self, I met someone who said they had a crazy woman inside, and when the crazy woman got out of control, it caused a disaster, because the crazy woman does everything she wants.

I had to know how to handle my crazy. She used to say, "*when the crazy woman gets out of me, the unfortunate woman makes a mess*", then she cried, she became neurotic and victimized herself.

When my madwoman dominated me, I was depressing, I had to take power over me, her weapon was my emotions, which altered and intensified me to the extremes, and when I realized it, I had to dominate it. What I did was not react and at the moment I managed the emotion (the anguish, the anxiety, the crying, the desolation) I analyzed it in my mind, until I felt that I could breathe normally, I reacted without aggression or altered. As a hypnotherapist, I used to say that this "crazy woman" was a lion that wanted to hunt you down, that at the least expected moment it was going to tear you apart, and if it caught you, you had a very bad time because it devastated you.

So, I was slowing down my mind, with that I began to manage my emotions and I began to have peace. It was difficult and very strong, but when a woman makes up her mind, she! does it¡.

The atmosphere in the house changed, you feel peace. My children said that they could not bear the tension before, that they wanted to leave the house and it was something that touched my heart, because they no longer felt that. When a woman changes her energy and love, everyone can feel it without it being said.

Adjust yourself to change to the same vibration. Yes, it took time for a change in attitude, but in the end, it benefited all of us because of the harmony in the home.

HOW DID I GET CERTIFIED AS A HYPNOTHERAPIST?

More than twenty years ago, I had finished studying accounting and was ready to start work but out of nowhere I got terrible depression with anxiety attacks.

Time passed and I realized that I couldn't get over this alone. I went to the doctor and was on medication for a little over two years, I expected the magical change announced in the commercials, in which the sun rises, and your life looks splendid again, but nothing happened. The doctor would give me my prescription in five minutes, and he would dispatch me, at the next appointment, I asked him ¿*when am I going to feel good*? He told me: "*don't expect that*, you have depression because your family had depression so you're going to deal with depression the rest of your life."

I left the place very upset, I never imagined that answer, I said to myself no, this cannot be happening to me, if I continue like this, I will die in one of those anxiety attacks or it will give me a cardiac attack.

I said to myself, I'm going to take a while to get out of this depression." I am very analytical, and I had my emotional agenda of how I felt from day to day. I pointed out at what time I had a panic attack and I saw what had caused it.

One day I went to a healing seminar where they presented hypnotherapy, I registered to attend the following weekend, and I drove hours away to attend. I had to drive alone, and I had panic attacks when I was driving, but interested me so much that I kept driving and I took the chance, and I loved it.

The content revolved around the management of stagnant emotions through relaxation and guidance, of course everything has a protocol and a procedure, what surprised me was that many of the techniques that they taught me, and now I had one more tool for my healing.

I perfected it by combining it with what I already knew so that it had faster effects. I dedicated myself fully to healing the emotions that had me stagnant and little by little I stopped taking the medicine, when the body heals on its own, it no longer needs the medicines. Every time I took the medicine, my hands would swell, and I told the doctor this. He already knew what he was doing (holistic treatments) and he told me to cut the pills little by little with a knife and adjust the dose, so I did. Until one day I no longer took anything.

Now I analyze it and I think that one plans, but God also plans for you. I think that since I already knew how to handle depression, I was able to go out and handle the divorce situation more effectively. Yes, I let myself be carried away by my emotions, but when I was at the lowest point, I could realize it and get up, when I made the decision and said that´s it, it was when everything changed in my favor, I stopped the pain and what follows, that life goes on…God wanted another path for me, and it was the one I followed.

I wrote a book on how to heal from depression, I hope you like it. I you have any questions I leave my e-mail:

elpoderdelasanacionestaenti@gmail.com
balanceemocional1@gmail.com

STRUGGLE FOR POWER

Our children loved us equally and wanted to continue living with both of us.

There is a power struggle between couples. You need allies, and who better to ally with than a son, a son who despises the father, which is very easy to achieve. All you must do is talk bad about the father and tell him how much he made you suffer so that he can be judge and executioner, to provoke conflict. I honestly thought about it, but I didn't do it, because I didn't want to hurt my children's hearts and then have regrets. They have their dad's love; I wasn't going to take it away from them by triumphing in my ego.

Situations made me angry, here the one who gets angry loses, and I was not going to lose what I love the most, which are my children, and I was not going to create dramas to break the harmony.

When we signed the divorce papers, it was clear to me that now that he was my partner, he was a partner that we had to look after the welfare of our children, that person is the father of my children and whether I want it or not, I will have to see him for the rest of my life, because there is still a lot to live, there are graduations, baptisms, birthdays, weddings, births... that we will have to celebrate together.

A NEW FAMILY REALITY

Everything changes, everything must be molded and readjusted. Let everything fall into place according to the new reality. I have to accept it. Nothing is or will ever be the same. If I set the example, it will be easier for my children to make the transition and the life adjustment that we will have to live from now on. I have to do it for my family with the expectation of creating harmony, and that living together will be beneficial for my children. I will not be the one to attack when the rules of coexistence, respect and honesty are not respected.

At the beginning, he was disconcerted and confused because he knew he had acted badly, he was afraid that I was going to tell them everything he knew, and he expected reproach, criticism and attacks. No, I was not going to do it, I had no right to that, he was no longer my partner and that belonged to the past. He wanted to act aggressively, defensively, but my cordial and serene attitude was enough for him to change his attitude to reach better agreements. This friendly attitude on my part confused him and he thought it was a sentimental approach, but it is far from reality.

He can be confused all he wants, because I am still firm, sure of my decision and I never sent signals of possible reconciliation. I have remained firm in my attitude and that made me feel good, because I could be close to him without provoking an argument. That has given me a lot of self-confidence.

I realized that the same time is spent in creating harmony or generating conflict and destruction, that can be for convenience, for that you need a lot of intelligence, because although we are no longer a couple, the children need their parents in harmony so they can live with both of them without dramas, this gives me peace and security to my children, they see that their family was not destroyed, only adjusted to a new reality.

WOMEN HAVE ALL THE POWER TO CHOOSE

The newly divorced woman faces a new conflict: how to face society and be respected? I was told, "now everyone will want you! you are going to be prey to harassment, ¡be careful!"

Every man fears rejection, he will never approach you until he sends you a flirtatious, approaching signal, and you respond to it. It's up to you if you approve, otherwise, he won't approach.

You have all the power to decide in your person, with whom you want to be, with whom you want to have a relationship, whether it is a friendship or a couple. The fact that someone wants to conquer you, doesn't mean that you have to accept it.

You have the right to say NO! when you don't agree or when you don't like it. Maybe you didn't know it, but now you know it, you are the one who decides what is going to happen. Do not respond to signals that can compromise you or get you in trouble, do not react impulsively, it can prevent you from getting a lot of headaches.

I ANNOUNCED MY SEPARATION

Because of my marital problems, divorce was a fact, and during the divorce process I withdrew from everything and everyone. My character had changed drastically, and I decided to withdraw from my friends and family.

I was absent for a long time from social media, only remaining active with the "nonprofit" who I had been serving for two years. At the corporation no one knew of my separation. Everyone assumed something was going on because of my sad look and my absence from meetings and personal events. I didn't say anything because I didn't want judgments, opinions, speculation, questions, or for them to feel sorry for me.

I thought and thought, how was I going to present myself to my people? I had already gone through my darkest nights and I had come out of it successfully. With what attitude was I going to present myself when they found out? What was I going to put on social networks? Do they have to know? I didn't want to make a circus out of my private life. I wanted privacy, I didn't want to give any explanation to anyone, and, besides, I didn't have to! I didn't say anything because I wanted privacy in a very hard and painful process.

I decided not to post anything on social networks, and I was only going to say that I was divorced and that is all and only when they asked me. If they asked me, I would say a firm yes in harmony without bitterness, without blaming anyone.

People were stunned, you could see it in their faces They never expected such a reaction from someone who just got divorced. They expected to hear complaints, drama, scandals; to destroy the other person in front of their eyes, and I did not do that.

In the organization that I belong to, I was continually active all the time. I never stopped because I was distracted and focused my mind on something different. The organization empowers women and at this time I needed to be busy.

They would see me sad, they would ask me, *"What's wrong with you*? Your look is incredibly sad", I would tell them, nothing, and because we were always very busy, we didn't go deep into the subject. I would do my work and I would retire, and it was like that for a long time until one day, one of them told me, *"I can't take it anymore, I have to ask you, what is happening to you*? you have changed so much, and we don't know what to think. I had not wanted to tell them anything, but at this point I knew they needed to know the truth. I told her I was getting divorced, she was speechless and said, *"I can't believe it, everything makes sense now,"* she continued, "*how could you go through all this by yourself*? It's unbelievable.

This has to be brought to the attention of the board of directors because they are very worried about you"; at the end of a meeting, they told me that they were very alarmed about me, they gave me the floor and I told them what was going on. There was silence and they began to hug me and tell me how sorry they were. I felt supported by them and I felt their unconditional friendship. It was a breakthrough.

From then on, I began to announce my divorce, I did it without drama or pain, to the people closest to me, such as my siblings, my parents, aunts, a few friends, and they could not believe it.

PEOPLE MEDDLE WHERE THEY ARE NOT CALLED

People would call me wanting to know how I was doing, and I would always tell them, “fine!" and they would answer me: “I thought a lot about talking to you since you are divorced, now, if you can tell....” Look, when we went to this place, I noticed... and I followed it, and I can even show you proofs! - ?Why are you telling me until now? - you are already divorced you shouldn’t care....

Yes, ¡it hurts! And ¡I got into an irrational rage! and I felt so bad, all day in my mind were coming and going ideas to claim one and another without being able to stop, I realized that I was falling into the same swamp from where I had left, and I did not want to go back. Drama, pain I took a deep breath and let it go, I would have done it to get revenge and leave him bad, but I was losing everything I had gained, and it was not worth it anymore.

BEING CORDIAL DOES NOT TAKE AWAY FROM BEING BRAVE

I have been divorced for quite some time now and I have seen that cordiality and good treatment have brought harmony to the home. The calmness and communication with the ex-partner have created a new bond with my children and with me, being able to live together when the occasion deserves it.

Drama that their dad is at home or not, every day is normal. I never make a comment out of place, I do not ask questions that don't interest me, I don't make bad faces or treat anyone badly, and that has worked very well for me. We feel better every day. We are a family that lives together, laughs, and works well. Sometimes, because we want to win over the other person's ego, things go wrong, and not with the result we want to obtain.

WHAT I GIVE, I RECEIVE

Now I want to invest in myself, just as I dedicated my time and attention to everyone. I want to plan what to do with my life, create and resume all the projects I stopped and have a start that refreshes my dignity, honor and fortifies my self-esteem.

It does not matter that he did not honor the relationship, it doesn't matter anymore his actions, nor how he treated me, nothing depends on him anymore, but on me. What he put in the basket that represents marriage, I put it in a river for the water to purify it. Now it is my turn to fill that basket with flowers. From now on I want to give myself what I deserve. To that person I gave my life and now I give him a worthy goodbye, not for him, but for me, after a marriage of many years I will not have bitterness in my heart for what I think I deserved and he did not give me, this makes me have control of my emotions and my life.

It is the way to save myself from the breakup. I discovered that the respect I have for the other person is what will give me peace, because what I give, I receive. Its like a mirror in which you see your reflection. Finish with dignity, when you finish with something you must do it well, even if you do not see it, people watch you and you will be in the opinion and judgment of others, because it is the concept, they will have of you, after how you acted; the way you do things reflects your personality.

¿WHY DOES RELATIONSHIPS STOP BEING HEALTHY?

Many couples who have ended in divorce have asked.

¿How is it possible that they ended up in this? ¿How is it that the relationship ended so badly? ¿But how is the couple going to end well? After having had so much suffering, resentment and even hatred: this is very stormy, especially when there are children involved.

I sought professional help and during therapy I understood many things and situations, I understood that, if I had acted differently, not as I did, it would have saved me a lot of time and suffering.

CHANGE BELIEFS

I couldn't handle it alone, the emotions were driving me crazy, I was in the middle of a crossroads. I wanted to start from the beginning, but I didn't know where the beginning was.

I had to seek professional help to guide me and find a way out, to put my mind at peace. I took cognitive therapy and found that beginning. *"Beliefs I had about marriage."*

Everything starts from here, I put a lot of illusion to a relationship that I thought was going to be for life, a deep-rooted belief that came from family. An idealization. It was a fixation.

Fixation, idealization and beliefs create a chemistry, which gets into your brain, and you don't realize how they affect your beliefs, your response to what happens to you because of what is in your mind. It is not the same to have an illusion to what you live outside and you see only what you want to see. When you wake up in reality, the truth is a shock.

I realized how our idealistic beliefs can corner us in our own mind and be a slave to yourself.

You sacrifice yourself for everyone, you work yourself to exhaustion, and you cover it with illusion, which is the best anesthesia not to feel the pain of disillusionment.

Everything changes, everything transforms, and love is no exception, you have had changes and you have not wanted to accept them, for not wanting to let go.

Many times, I felt the freedom of being me, and I felt disconnected from him, I felt at ease, I felt good, time passed and when I saw myself freer, I was afraid and I got hooked again, now I see it and I analyze it, I submitted myself, I did not want to accept that my soul wanted to change, how many times I ignored it, I don't know!

When I realized this, it was easier to agree, just as everyone changes, I could also change, give myself the opportunity to be free and dream of a different world than the one I had imposed on myself, maybe because I felt safe.

When I accepted my freedom, something in me was transformed, it was as if that enthusiastic girl came back to life, I felt that a weight fell off my shoulders, I felt a freedom that I began to recognize and always rejected to fulfill a promise that had been broken for a long time and it had not been because of me.

!I felt happy, what a beautiful freedom¡, everything was so easy, I felt that I was the owner of myself, I felt that I could conquer the world and everything was for me. I resumed my projects, I felt my excitement vibrate, the days were so short, I could not reach the day of so much that I had to schedule, blessed freedom, what a great happiness and for it to arrive you just have to let go.

RELEASE

Do not turn an individual into a god or put them on a pedestal, no matter who they are, my partner, my children, my parents, a friend. As women we create very strong and deep connections with the ones we love and give them time, affection, passion, and sometimes we put them on an altar.

I give so much, I forget that people have free will and can choose any path, like turning away from one, it's a law of life. Our connections are so intense and beliefs so deep, that they cause attachments that chain us and we believe that people can't fail us.

THEY LEAVE BECAUSE THEY DON'T KNOW HOW TO APPRECIATE YOU

[6]A woman knows that her value is not money, nor physical appearance, but the very essence of the person who seeks her equal.

Her values distinguish her, her intelligence amazes, her truthfulness, tenacity and audacity is her strength. This is valued by a man with the same principles and feelings; if he does not have the same qualities, he will not be able to see and appreciate them and will have to leave your life. If he leaves, let him go because he will not provide you with the same things that you give or ask for, such as loyalty, values, truthfulness and respect.

Understanding that life is a wonderful game to enjoy, we have to learn the basic rules, and knowing how to let go in time is one of them.

---

[6] Lucia Martine. Mujeres exitosas en AA

INTEGRITY

Integrity means doing good, even if no one sees you.

When you are a person of integrity and you cling to something that can no longer be, your integrity screams at you to let it go, you know deep down that it has to end. Your instinct tells you, it guides you and your integrity speaks to you and that everything will be okay, you just have to let go and return to your center.

Integrity speaks of who you are and when I do what I say, my actions speak louder than words. When you listen to your intuition, it will always lead you to integrity which is peace of mind. Making the best and accurate decision will make you happy and it is the truth that makes you a person of integrity.

DIGNITY

Dignity gives you a sense of fulfillment, satisfaction and self-esteem that enhances your personality. Dignity honors people especially when you are going through a divorce.

UNCERTAINTY

If uncertainty floods you and eats you up inside and does not let you see the reality of who you are living with, look beyond what you see and analyze what you feel and you will find you, your truth. Do not be devastated, you are not alone, you have you.

I WORKED ON MY HEALING

If analyzing my beliefs is going to give me peace and I have to work on it I will work on it and achieve it. Every day I recorded videos of therapies and listened to them over and over and over again until I felt calm and peaceful. Sometimes I lasted up to a month with the same lesson, I did not leave anything incomplete until I found in me every emotion that hammered my soul, I studied it, analyzed it, understood how it had affected me and how I could adjust it for my good.

It took me a long time, but day by day I felt better. I worked on each emotion to the maximum until I found the truth. They say that the truth will set you free and yes, every day is a truth that you discover. All beliefs have to be readapted to change for my benefit.

¿WHY DOES THE OTHER ONE GET EVERYTHING THEY WANT?

Some women ask me, ¿why is the other one more successful than me? ¿why couldn't I keep him and conquer him? ¿ why is he now doing with her what I asked him so much to do with me and my children? ¡it's not fair! The other one has achieved what ¡I never could!

The other means entertainment, variety, novelty, taste. No one can stop a relationship between two adult people if they want to live a romance.

And even if the woman is the best wife, the one who wants to cheat will always find a way to do it, this will make him more appetizing, because it creates more adrenaline that causes him more excitement, makes him feel more desired, he feels like a superman.

For the mistress, it becomes a challenge, she has to take him to live with her and be the ideal partner.

Here are some details:

The mistress does not make any drama, she is forbidden to quarrel, otherwise she loses her lover.

No punishments, no reproaches,

No absurd arguments, only pleasure.

She does not criticize him, he is perfect.

She admires him all the time, she pampers him. He is the best thing that has ever happened to her.

She always looks for ways to make the bond between them stronger and that nothing and no one can break it.

She never stops talking to him and if that happens, she is quick to make him happy in the best possible way.

She is the best friend of him

She never argues. She can't afford that luxury, because if she does it, she loses his admiration, and what's worse could happen she can lose everything.

There are up and down, but she always finds the balance. She always must be on his side, for her it's a life investment.

She hears him. She creates deep communication. She doesn't abuse or accuse him.

She doesn't find fault with him. In every defect he has, she brings out a quality in him and everything he does, she does it super well.

She pampers him. She finds phrases specially made for him from the moment he wakes up, she spoils him making him feel that he is super special. Getting him to share his opinions, expressing his deepest feelings without feeling judged.

She nurtures him.

They re-educate him like puppies, they don't reward him until he does a good trick. They stimulate him to meet their expectations, they treat him so special until he does what they ask of him and they release something new to them until they get where they want, and the man is tamed again.

¿Why the change?

¿What went wrong with them?

Their relationship is as a couple, a partner, friends. The wife plays the role of kind of mother when they married instant to be a husband he wants to be served, as child of hers.

Their relationship is as a couple, a partner, friends. The wife plays the role of kind of mother when they married instant to be a husband he wants to be served, as child of hers.

Usually, after a divorce, many of the women feel a lot of pain and frustration, especially after having found out that their ex-husbands helped the new partner with the house chores, picking up the new wife´s children at school, helped with the her kid´s homework, cooked, washed the dishes, etc., and said lamenting: why in so many years of marriage he never helped me and now is a perfect husband comes and fulfills all of her demands without hesitation, and the hell begins for the ex-wife.

I have been shocked, knowing what I know now. When I was young I would have liked to have received guidance from my parents about what it is to have a real and not a fictitious relationship, to be partners and spouses, to be loyal to one, not to lose myself, and without fear of losing what really matters, it impacts not to have set a limit when our elementary rights are exceeded and to have been tolerant because we are taught to look for love and be slaves of that love, to look for a male disguised as Prince Charming, who trains you to treat him as a king, and not a responsible and loyal man.

Instead of looking for love, we must know how to look within ourselves what are the gifts that God gave us, develop them and be professional in that, create an economy that makes me self-sufficient and create a savings, be a person economically and emotionally independent, not to fall into codependence, to see true love with different eyes, the pure love that does exist at other levels and attract a human being worthy of a love that is at the height of oneself, and that is when true love will appear, and if you want it, it will be for life.

NEVER BETRAY YOURSELF TO PLEASE OTHERS.

This phrase has touched my soul, I have felt it, lived it and acted on it. Out of habit you always fall into the same mistake, you do everything for everyone but yourself.

ʕYOU ARE A SEXUAL OBJECT?

When the relationship is for pleasure or convenience, and not for love, a relationship of domination and submission is created, where they become sexual objects to each other.

At the same time, they become a magnet that attracts people with the same energetic sexual vibration, people get closer just to get pleasure, it is a bond that they create, many people wonder why they always attract one type of person, feeling empty, used, and tired that they reach total exhaustion.

This causes frustration because they always lose out, in time and money, they end up disillusioned, they only attract birds of prey looking for advantages, seducing, and making them believe they are the best, until they get bored and leave for another victim. The more sex you have, the stronger the bond becomes each day, reaching lust.

When you have sex you create energetic links that connect between sexual partners with the partners of the partners you have had, creating a network of energy exchanges with individuals you have never met, nor will you meet, because they were or are partners of the partner of the other partner you do not know, but you will have communication at the energetic level (perception of moods, emotions that you did not have before, tastes for things you did not like before, you can be very hungry and you just ate, etc.), it is as if you have other personalities that you cannot understand, but you perceive the link created at the energetic level is exchanged, permeates and melts in you, without suspecting the energetic contamination to which you expose yourself.

After a while you are a magnet, attracting toxic people. The negative energy of each person permeates the other and is the one that dominates, making you change your previous programming and having a drastic and illogical personality change.

Beliefs, values, judgments, and actions will again be reprogrammed by the energetic contamination of the other person. Although he considers himself assertive, cheerful, he becomes apathetic, dissatisfied, and feels very tired by the low dense and dark vibration to which he is subjected, this makes him feel lost.

The unfaithful husband can be very clever in covering his infidelity, but the energy is felt and although the wife does not know anything she perceives and senses it, she feels a strange change, an attitude that although he wants to hide, the woman realizes it. The sexual energy of the other woman is opposite to that of the wife and although they feel each other, they repel each other.

There are already two women opposite sexual energies in the energy field of the man, the two women create energetic connections among them. Each one create unique connections depends of the relationship they want with the man creating a whirlwind of passions between the three. Each woman has her well-programmed objectives, the wife wanting stability for her home and children, the other wanting to destroy whoever opposes her to her will, the dominion of the married man.

Between the two women, begins the rivality that becomes war to win although the wife does not know it, only intuits it, all this happens in the energy field.

The other woman has the advantage of having the man as an accomplice because she is the lover and between the two play to have an affair and the wife is the enemy of the two. One to the other they put their conditions and rules to not be discovered, this deception hooks the man with adrenaline for the passion, which excites him to have a lover.

The man begins to be dominated and subtly reprogrammed, the man loses the admiration and respect towards his wife. The efforts and dedication that she dedicated to the home are annulled and the devaluation towards the woman he admired becomes aggression. Now he brings the concepts and ideas of the new woman, which is a new tuning in him generating a very drastic change.

He is very confused and sometimes when he sees everything lost, he tries again to win over his wife just to know that he does not lose her at all and to feel secure with himself.

Many times, the wife is determined to leave the relationship, but she does not have willpower, his presence dominates her, and it always ends in the same game as his.

Divorced women start off as wives and end up being lovers and now they play on the other side; for many it is devastating, but they cannot avoid it, passion overwhelms them. The emotional relationship continues because it is a physical separation; the energetic relationship continues because it has not been cut off.

I knew that my relationship was no longer working and was very exhausting, but, even so, when I made the decision to end the relationship, let the time pass and I came back and wrapped myself again, I returned to my decision and ended.

I knew that I had to go through that energetic process for the relationship to end and I knew that if I'm doing it, it was going to be the real end, the end forever and I thought about it a lot until one day I said I'm over it, I made the power energetic cut and it was all over, that's where the emotional relationship ended.

I had done this therapy with people as hypnotherapist before, but I had never done something like this for me, I knew it was decisive, but when I experienced it, it was as if the emotion had disappeared, I felt the other person was an alien to me because the only thing that united us was the energetic bond, trust and intimacy were a thing of the past, so this was the end. If you want a cut off this energetic membrane, whether you are a man or a woman, contact me and we can do the therapy. Remember you have to be well determined that everything is over.

Send me an email to:

Balanceemocional1@gmail.com
elpoderdesanacionestaenti@gmail.com

¿IS HE, MY SOULMATE? ¡THAT'S WHY I CAN'T LEAVE HIM!

When you have a toxic relationship, that person interconnects the subject at the cellular memory level, especially the man where he is constantly bombarded with ideas and feelings that confuse and depress him. Calling him, creating restlessness to go looking for her, that is why it is exceedingly difficult to end a toxic relationship.

Each sexual partner creates energetic bonds that are active and nourished through their vital and sexual energy dominating the will of the weaker one.

Stormy relationships are created by people without values, poorly educated and codependent.

People who do not know about this, and feel an extraordinarily sexual strong connection, that dominate their will power, although they know that the relationship is very wearing and negative, they think they found their soulmate, because you cannot leave that person, they do not know that this person is nourished by their vital energy.

This makes him weaker and weaker and more vulnerable; it can only cut off the energetic membranes that are created when there is a sexual relationship.

REGAINING A SENSE OF BELONGING AND SECURITY

"You are a being created by divine right, because before your parents thought of you, God already had you by his side. You are stardust containing all that exists in the universe, so you can create whatever you wish." Ask and it will be given to you.

I am convinced that all of us, at some point in our lives, have felt an emotional void. ¿What is an emotional void? You feel an emotion that turns into a feeling of great sadness and a great sense of loneliness. ¡You know that there is something missing that you need to feel complete, but you cannot identify it with certainty! You feel the need for affection, loyalty, love, approval, and a sense of belonging.

Knowing that these feelings exist, you feel the need to experience them. When you open yourself to the decision to accept and consciously receive those feelings, the universe gives you permission to experience that feeling, and it is as if the breeze of dawn comes and fills everything in its path with softness, arrives without warning permeating your whole being, awakening all your senses, reprogramming that magical code that only the universe knows and that is love and acceptance. This inevitably leads to creating and reaffirming a right of belonging, because you are in this world to be, live, feel and experience happiness.

SOCIAL CHANGE

I wanted something different for myself; inside I felt a dissatisfaction and I knew that was what I was missing, I wanted a different social environment, to have new friendships, to attend different events that had a different purpose, I really enjoyed theater, music, photography, painting, writing, sports, and even being part of non-profit organizations of my interest.

I am attracted to people who are dedicated to an art, who have a passion for what they do. Wanting was not enough and I had to take action to get my interest moving. I asked God to show me the way. I didn't know how to find what I was interested in or where to start, "I wanted to get out of my mental, cultural and social poverty."

Once when I was driving, I heard on the radio that if you want to be an entrepreneur, the same entrepreneurs gave you classes on how to start a business, I was very interested and I went to all the courses they gave, I started to connect with different people, I became a volunteer in schools, city events, non-profit corporations that helped the development of Latina women and helped me grow as a person.

GIVE YOURSELF SELF-LOVE TO ACHIEVE TRUE LOVE

¿Does unconditional and true love really exist? Yes, ¡ it does exist! and you can give it without any restrictions.

¿To whom can we give this love without limits? ¡ Ourselves! ¡Why do we always give ourselves to others and leave ourselves for last! ¿Why do we seek acceptance from people, and we do not accept ourselves as we are, and we dislike ourselves?

There is no one more genuine and special than you ¡and no one can deny that! And to love yourself, the first thing is the acceptance of yourself, recognize yourself (PHYSICAL BODY) but more than the body is your ESSENCE, it is not tangible, you cannot see it, but you can feel it, and your life's MISSION that only you can fulfill, God gives it to you to give meaning to your life.

God gives you everything, He sends you here and now to live an extraordinary experience. It is up to you to decide how you want to experience it, it could be a nightmare, or it could be wonderful.

At birth, we are born with everything, you are perfect and unrepeatable, you have the five senses to explore yourself and the world. You are like a magic box that you can fill with everything you want and can make of yourself. You have a box of tools that God gave you, you just have to recognize them and for that you have to pay attention and listen to your mind and heart because there is the key to what you are and what gifts you have to make sense of life, ¿what do you like to do?, ¿what are you great at?, ¿are you super-fast with your mind?,¿ do you like to read?, ¿write?, ¿cook?, ¿swim?, ¿play basketball?, ¿design dresses?,¿chemistry?, ¿Physics?, ¿Mathematics?, ¿Do you have an extraordinary imagination?, ¿Do you draw? etc., here nobody comes with a disadvantage if you do, you´ll find the way to do it. Everyone who is born brings a special gift impregnated in the DNA, you just have to discover it in you, you have the same hours of the day that everyone has, wherever you want and it is just a matter of applying yourself in what you are going to do with your gifts and how you are going to develop it. Open your mind, dream, imagine reaching your blessing.

People who close in on themselves are lost because they look outside what they have inside and close their mind.

[7] *"God gives us all water, but He doesn't tube it, so you have to know where your water is and you have to do the work to make it come to you".*

There is a story that moved me to my soul, it was the story of the basketball player Kobe Bryant: it is about a boy who wanted to be the most successful basketball player in the world, and he succeeded, he already had his gift in his blood, in his mind, in his spirit, in his DNA. He knew that to achieve his dream he had to be the best, because there were already leaders in basketball, and he had to work more than 100%. If they asked him to arrive at eight in the morning, he was there at five and stayed after practice. He had passion.

Passion fills you with energy that gives you strength to achieve your dreams, it is when you connect your soul and the soul of the universe.
¿How do you do it? By dedicating time to do what you love, even if you don't get paid for it. Your gifts scream at you to bring them out, the sign is that you can't stop thinking that you have to do it; famous people are a clear example in the passion they dedicate to everything they are inclined to be.

---

[7] Los cuatronados Oscar Coate AA

Feeling, experiencing, enjoying, some like swimming like Michael Phelps, others like golf like Tiger woods, ballet like Misty Copeland, music like Natalia Lafourcade, science like Marie Curie who was a chemist who discovered radioactivity and won the first Nobel Prize in Physics in 1903. Ophra Gail Winfrey Philanthropy, author, actress, producer, media executive, creator of her magazine and launched her TV NETWORK OWN.

All these honorable people had what we have: time, a gift and a mission to fulfill. Each of them was driven by a passion, they had it fixed in their minds that they had to do it.

When you discover your passion, dedicate the time it requires, and when you get to the point where you feel you're being fulfilled is when you will be blessed. All the roads to your dream will open and God or the universe, whatever you want to call it, will connect you to the essence of the universe and everything is given to you, but you have to put in the work, effort and dedication, that only depends on you.

When you give the best of you, that is true love because you give yourself to what you love the most and you must give it to the universe.
When you have already done the work, you will reach the glory and the economic level that your effort deserves, you put the zeros you want.

When you expect people to do for you, to try for you, and you do nothing, you close your mind and you lose your blessing, you feel a dissatisfaction, discomfort, nothing fills you, nothing satisfies you, it is an emptiness that is not filled with anything.

Dissatisfaction always seeks relief and seeks something that alters the senses so as not to feel a thirst that is never filled. When it alters the senses, you feel it as a delight, and you are inclined to vices.

¡Many people have never been able to silence the voice of the soul, they do not know what it is! ¿Where does it come from? and they fill the body with alcohol and drugs, it calms them for a while, but that becomes an addiction, addiction is a vice of pleasure that the more you give it the more it demands from you. Until you lose control of your life. That pleasure, the universe gives it to you for free, you seek it indirectly in vices, leisure, and boredom in life.

The sign that you have not found your passion manifests itself in annoyance, apathy. Apathy is the worst because nothing interests to you, nothing surprises you, nothing moves you and because of laziness you ignore your own being and submit it to your will, trapping the spirit in slavery.

No one will force you to do anything, because only you can recognize yourself, no one else and only you know what you want. God will not force you to do the work that corresponds to you, but you will never find your grace and you will be unhappy. Unhappy in love is killing your truth with false emotions.

One of them is the pleasure to sexuality, to sex without love and that is rooted to the deepest part of the soul, you are not happy, and you do not make anyone happy. Vices only bring shame and dishonor, you create a new arrogant, narcissistic personality, an ego that is exceedingly difficult to tame.

Nobody can change a behavior so rehearsed and learned by the deviation of the self, the only way is to touch bottom and pay attention to your life, nobody is going to get you out of any vice created by yourself, but to look inside oneself. You fell there because of ignorance, now with this you know it: ¡get rescued!

True love, the genuine one, comes when you have fulfilled your mission in life, or if you are already on the way to your achievements.

Many people complain about not finding love and that is because the person is not ready, because if not, he or she never gets to develop and focus on his or her mission.

Most young couples get married without knowing who they are marrying, because they have not reached emotional and physical maturity, nor personal development (mission in life) and end up in a life-changing failure. Many of the people who have separated in the end focus on being alone and undertake their dreams that they abandoned because they paid attention to the partner, who in the end was not the ideal partner for their personal purposes.

If you have not found your passion yet, just wait. Search in you, what do you want from life and life will answer you with inspiration, it will awaken in you something that you thought you had forgotten, the restlessness and the ability that you always had since you were a child. Wait, discover and when you find it, ask the universe if this is what is true, and the universe will answer you and you will know it.

If you are in a relationship, give yourself the time to develop what you have always wanted to do and prioritize it until you find your lost dreams. ¡GOOD LUCK!

BRING OUT YOUR VIRTUES AND SKILLS

Happiness does not depend on a partner or person, since you are complete you know what makes you happy. When you have a partner, it is only a complement to you. Your life is terribly busy with work, children, and husband, but still, the inner restlessness of what you love and what you have always wanted to do is not silent, it asks for your attention.

Your spirit asks you to develop your gifts, to bring out your virtues and abilities, that idea, that taste that you have stuck in the mind of your soul, even if it seems irrational and crazy to people, but for you it is true. You have to do it because it has already become an obsession, they are ideas that you cannot stop thinking about.

When you do not fulfill your task, you feel anxious, you want to eat something, and you don't know what? You try and try, and nothing tastes good, you feel everything tasteless, you feel thirsty, and nothing quenches it, and you already have thirty pounds more. Until you finally make your taste come true, you feel satisfied, you enter in balance, peace comes to your mind, your heart is happy and full of happiness, you finally listen to your inner voice, the one that always spoke to you but that you were reluctant to listen to.

I DISCOVERED ONE OF MY GIFTS LATE IN LIFE

As a child, I always wanted to swim and never could. I had an image in my mind where I swam. I don't know if it was a beautiful lagoon or in the sea. Every time I remembered it, I had a warm feeling of total fulfillment when I submerged in the water.

Swimming, for me, was a delight, so I wanted my children to learn to swim at a professional level. During summer vacation, I registered my son when he was 7 years old for swimming lessons. Being at the facility, the attendant informed me that the child could take the class alone, I was thrilled with the idea, it was the first time I could be unsupervised with my youngest child, I was free, free in many years, and I thought out loud and said, “what am I going to do with me?” and the young man at registration said, “you can take the class at the same time as your child.”

I was overcome with excitement, and of course I registered. I was super excited because all my life I wanted to learn. Of course, I registered. I was super excited because all my life I wanted to learn to swim, it was my dream come true.

On the first day of class, I noticed that all the ladies who brought their children were acquaintances of mine, they couldn’t help but look at me with surprise when they saw me in my swimsuit ready to learn and asked me, “aren’t you embarrassed?”, and I said, “embarrassed why?” - “Well because you are already old”, I replied, “No! all my life I have wanted to learn to swim, it’s a dream come true!”

I loved the classes, I laughed a lot, I met two ladies with whom I teamed up, we were always together in the pool. When the instructors, who were very athletic and fit young men, taught us the swimming techniques and we started practicing we almost drowned, one leg floated and the other didn't, we all ended up twisted, we made fun of each other; we didn't know how to control our bodies in the water, but with practice we managed it, it was very fun and de-stressing.

I think it was one of the most fun times of my life. I was that little girl who always wanted to swim, I did something I always wanted to do that gave me a lot of happiness.

The ladies would watch us and ask me, "how do you feel?" and I could only manage to tell them, "¡¡¡super happy!!!" By the sixth week we were crossing the entire pool, as a plus it helped me get in shape.

They also stopped me at the exit of the facilities to ask me if it was difficult, I answered: "at the beginning, but I see it as fun." The last week of classes we had to jump off the diving board. I had not gone to the last class and some people told me, "don't jump! what if you don't get out", I just thought that if I didn't do it, I would regret it all my life and I was not going to miss this opportunity. When I got ready to jump off the diving board, I asked the lifeguard and my companions -

somewhat joking and telling the truth - if I didn't come up in a few seconds to call 911 and news channel 34.

The instructor was concerned about me, he was watching me very closely and that made me feel confident and ¡I jumped! It was a wonderful experience, when I got into the pool, I opened my eyes, I saw the depth of the pool, it looked super blue, and I felt like a mermaid in the depth.... and an unknown feeling of fullness, then, the water did its job, my body rose to the surface, when I got out, everyone was expectant of my triumphant exit, suddenly everyone was shouting at me: *Swim, swim, swim to the end*! It was beautiful, if I had had the opportunity to swim in my childhood, I know I would have been a professional swimmer.

Fears of the unknown paralyze us, but they say that through fear there is the magic of power, which makes your dreams come true. When you have many achievements, you strengthen your soul and spirit with experiences that fill you with fulfillment.

All this makes you have a firm, strong, empowered personality with self-mastery and control. It could even be compared to the pleasures of love that no longer dominate you or make you lose control as before, nor do you become obsessed.

BlendEssence IS BORN

I kept discovering different passions of mine and my line of skin oils was born and I named it:

'BLENDESSENCE" I have always had a very deep connection with nature, I believe that the earth gives us everything to survive and heal.

I never used creams of any kind for my skin because I didn't need them, but, when I came of age, I had very dry skin and I felt very desperate, I started to use the creams that are on the market and they didn't work as I expected, I was not used to the chemicals and preservatives most creams contain, they made me very itchy, and even worse, their aroma. I couldn't stand it.

Since I was very young, I have had a strong interest in Egyptian culture. I loved it and always read about its history and cultural aspects. I thought "*I had been Egyptian in my other life.*" One day I saw the broadcast of a documentary in which they had located a sunken ancient ship, more than a thousand years old, and inside they found carafes with aromatic oil that were in very good condition and perfectly sealed.

This gave me the idea of preparing essential oils for my skin. It was hard work of research, testing and practice. I experimented for a long time, investing money in supplies, time and effort. Every day I obtained better results, I experimented first with myself, then with my family and finally with close friends. During the process I experimented with different skin types, seeing the good results on our face and body, people asked me what I put on my skin, they saw me looking more youthful with a tanned tone. After a while I started to sell it because people asked me for it, it had been recommended to them.

I discovered that when you have passion for something and more so for nature, it responds to you.

The formula is fabulous, after so much time I am ready to launch my line of skin oils, especially to nourish the face (FACIAL OIL) and neck, an oil for the eye area (EYE OIL), for under eye bags because it is the thinnest skin on the whole body and is where water is deposited and can become stagnate due to lack of circulation, the oil moisturizes the skin to such a degree that it prevents wrinkles.

I have a lot of faith in my products, I prepare them with natural products without preservatives, the skin recognizes the natural ingredients and absorbs them super-fast without leaving greasy residues. I learned that when you do something with passion, dedication and love, the universe responds and gives you wonderful results.

My skin oils can be found in my website.

www.blendEssenceOnline.com

WORKS FOR YOU, AND YOUR EXPECTATIONS CHANGE

The masked sexuality that the media sells us, enters our homes as entertainment daily, it has practically been imposed on us as a dominion in our being. The woman is emotional and appreciates more the details, not everything for her is intercourse, but rather to feel in love and the physical contact such as a hug, a kiss or even non-sexual intimacies like just enjoying a good movie together. The pleasure and well-being she desires is to fill her life with pleasurable things so that she is not begging for love.

When you nurture yourself with activities that you like, your expectations of looking for love decrease and they no longer have the same concern in you, the best way to revalue yourself is to work for you, because you will discover the potential you have. In everything you do, focus, do the best you can, make the most of your time. Do something for yourself every day, commit to yourself every day and when you least expect it, you will find yourself satisfied, fulfilled, different, empowered and you will see that your effort was worth it, and that it is ¡all for you!

I AM UNLUCKY IN LOVE

؟You are unlucky in love? ؟ you are looking for a partner in vain? ؟you do not find anything for you? In the universe everything is in order, you have not worked on developing your gifts that fill you with assertiveness, positive energy and empowerment, therefore you do not have the developed energy to love in fullness.

When you develop your gifts and apply them, many tests appear that you must overcome.

When you work on your life mission, life tests you to create a strong, assertive character, which will be part of your personality, if you do not start there is no process, no lifeline to work on.

If you keep quiet or do not want to make it your mission or life project, and your attitude begins to change, you become apathetic, angry, envious of the love of others and think you need to love. You long for an ideal love and look for a partner in vain.

Your spirit knows well what it wants and what it has to do. Finding a partner at this time is one more obstacle to your personal development.

You may find a very beautiful partner, seductive, that moves you the floor, good sex, maybe at that moment you calm the sexual anxiety that you carry, but, in the long run, does not satisfy your being completely, that is, you do not feel complete, because you have neither the vibration nor the personality, nor the life project, nor the attitude that attracts a true affinity. You will find people in development who are looking for someone to rescue them, incomplete, distracted, who have no purpose in life and do not want to work on anything, they are people who are looking for someone to distract them, give them attention, they get bored and leave, they only leave you confused and make you lose your way.

¿What do you need to find the ideal person for you, develop a vibration that gives you personality and that a partner with your vibration is attracted and comes into your life?

Everything in the universe is a process, and to get to this you have to comply with the universal laws, you have to have done good things for others, have overcome all the obstacles and trials that life has put or given you to have a high vibration and have a captivating personality where you are a magnet to attract everyone with your light.

YOUR PASSION SCARES YOU

I already mentioned that I have always written and that I am a hypnotherapist. I mention it because this experience that I write below happened years ago, but I remembered and wanted to mention it in this book.

Mara was a young academic professional, very quiet, very serious, but she had a very strong sentimental disillusionment. Her fiancé broke off the engagement with her. ¡ She was devastated! She was very depressed and asked me to help her get rid of this depression. As a hypnotherapist I consulted her. It took a series of sessions and her beliefs and habits were discovered, etc.

We met and talked and the advice for her was connect to her inner self, discover, and find her passions!

In one session she had a "déjà" vu which is about the feeling of having previously gone through an experience, when in reality it is the first time we have lived it. She recognized herself dancing tango, she knew that she loved tango, but she was terrified to think what they were going to think of her. She told me I am a professional with great respect, how can I see myself dancing so sensual.

I know you are a professional, but it is something you learned, it is an instruction to be a professional. There are professions that you are passionate about and that fill your life, but there are also personal passions that move your being. You are very shy, but that doesn't mean you don't have that spark that moves you with passion.

After a while, I received a phone call, it was Mara, where she told me: “I dared to do it, I’m in a tango school and I feel myself, I feel very sure of myself, it is as if I felt that my body vibrates in all its power, and I feel empowered, it is a feeling of freedom within me and it makes me feel complete. I cannot explain it. If I had known this, I would have done it without thinking, but I felt so insecure I was scared to even think about it. but I left my insecurity and shyness aside.”

She dared to do what her spirit asked of her and she knew she had to do it because she never stopped thinking about it, feeling it and longing for it. Nothing becomes real, until you work on it. ¡Connect to you, discover and find your passion! She dared to do something different. Nothing becomes so real, until you work at it.

YOU HAVE TO KNOW HOW TO WAIT FOR LOVE

If you want to find the partner that makes you feel happy, you have to know how to wait for him or her to come at the right time. So do not look for partners, even if you feel loneliness, it can confuse you more and end up worse than you started, because you can trap yourself and you will not be able to get out of a relationship that you acquired by confusion. It's possible that the person does not fulfill your expectations and leaves you emptier.

While you wait, connect to nature to nourish yourself with positive energy so that the wait does not become long.

SEXUAL CONNECTION WITH LOVE

We know that we are spiritual beings living an earthly experience and that we are pure energy, sexual energy is one of the most intense, pleasurable and creative energies of the human being.

When a relationship begins, an energetic connection begins. When the couple has a sexual union, that is where the energetic connection begins because they merge with each other.

When two people who love each other come together, their energetic vibration rises to the same level. They are two very similar energies, that when they look at each other in a mirror they see their image reflected as one, even if it is the energy of the other. They must have very similar beliefs, education, ideals.

When there is a sexual relationship there is a union of energies that nourish each other feeling full and satisfied, wanting to be together all the time, this energy makes them vibrate, they become more enthusiastic, cheerful, they are happy all the time, they are very friendly, positive and have many projects together. They feel that life has given them everything.

TO MY BEST TEACHER

I thank God for having given me this experience, I know that without his support I would not have gotten out of this. I met, I managed to overcome the most terrible adversities that anyone can imagine, I learned great lessons and you realize that you came to this world to face great battles, nobody but you can fight them.

You have to make the most drastic and decisive decisions alone, because God respects your free will, and you just have to take the paths and reins of your life. This taught me to respect the decisions of others. No one is forced to leave their path to bow to yours if it is not their wish, you learn to live alone, and you embrace your freedom. There is nothing more beautiful than freedom. That you can be you, it is wonderful to find this gift and privilege in you and it is more beautiful to live with your partner when they love each other, when there is no longer this, you learn to let go.

How hard it is to let go of so many years of coexistence, the memories that suddenly come to you and make you shiver, as if to test you if you have overcome the experience. The fact that you make the decision to move on does not mean that you will not have bittersweet memories, and that you will not have a memory or a photo where you were happy with that person who wanted to leave your life, you learn to live with that and not get hooked and torment you.

Be careful with the memory, the memory brings mixed feelings that shake you all, but that is normal. After so many years together, it is impossible and irrational to think that the mind can empty itself, empty memories, feeling from one moment to another. Get used to the memories, that sometimes they will come to touch your distracted mind and they will leak. Do not get excited, do not get hooked or pay much attention to them, because if you do, they will give you a drag that will throw you on the ground: Get used to that, little by little it will happen to you.

At first it is very difficult and depressing, the loss hurts you. People ask me: "*¿And don't you feel lonely*? "He answered them: "*yes*" *¿and it doesn't hurt*? They keep telling me. Sure, *¡it did!* It hurts, I am not made of steel, but I know that I worked hard for this, that it helped me accept my reality and work with what I have, and that is me and nobody else but me.

But ¡beware! being alone, you can fall into temptations and betray yourself and divert your way to what you really want to achieve for yourself.

MY PRESENT TO YOU

I did field research to get all the necessary information, the opinions and experiences of many women guided me. This was one of the reasons that prompted me to write the book.

Talking with women who were in a marriage for years opened my eyes and I realized that we are not prepared emotionally or financially to face a loss at the time, either from the couple, because they are widowed, divorced or live-in free union and separated.

Some do not know how to find love or how to maintain a lasting relationship, the latter involves many circumstances, and I took the liberty of detailing other people's situations because, although it was not my situation or experience, it could be someone else's and the purpose is to guide to people who are in emotional crisis with dysfunctional marriages or toxic relationships.

THE PURPOSE OF THIS BOOK

I see my hands. I have a ring on that I bought when I had just got married. In December, I would have been married for 30 years, but that's not the case anymore, I was already divorced.

The day of my supposed anniversary I saw the date, the memories came vaguely, but they no longer mattered to me, they no longer caused pain, they were only memories, that day I saw myself with a friend and I told her that "this day I would be celebrating my 30th anniversary", and answered me:

"I can't believe you have that attitude, someone else in your place would be dead in tears", I smiled and said: "I already suffered the crying and pain

to reach this state of emotional balance, I already cried a lot, I already faced it that nobody can imagine, I suffered a very painful loss, I had to face myself, take my share of responsibility in this relationship, face my beliefs and my fears; they took me out of my comfort zone from one day to the next, feeling helpless , betrayed, abandoned, but it is over ... I asked God to help me because I felt that I could not overcome so much pain and He helped me overcome it. "

I wrote this book to help women who are going through this process, a process that I had to live alone, but you already have a guide here.

I want you to know that everything happens, everything changes and what one day caused you so much pain, at some point it will become part of the past and you will think: "*wow this is life, this is glory!*"

Feeling so good being in harmony with your emotions is being in heaven living on earth. In this book you will find very strong life lessons that are experienced in a marital breakdown. Each stage I lived, felt, analyzed, and worked on emotionally until I felt that I had healed her and let her go.

Some lessons were more difficult than others, but I insisted on my healing. I did not want to be one of those bitter people, who are crying for the loss of a marriage in which I could no longer be happy.

I remember that, years before, I had read the book The Alchemist by Pablo Coelho, and I remember that the protagonist of the story had traveled the world, and at the end of the story returned to the starting point. This is how it happened to me, I had to return to myself, which was the starting point.

I also remember that one day I was walking at the Autonomous University of Mexico and I saw it and thought how much I loved being there, I in the center of my being knew that I was born to be someone great, at the time I felt freedom and a fullness in me, something told me that I did not have to get married and I had to put all my efforts to achieve everything I aspired to, such as doing a university degree, being independent.

At that time, I was studying and working. I do not know at what point in my life I forgot, maybe, it was when love crossed my way, that love that makes me feel so special, and makes me lose my mind, you give yourself and give everything for love… ¿what is everything? You everything: your time, your ideals, your dreams, your complete being to get to have a family, next to the man you love.

That family depends on you for everything, and you don't have time for yourself to develop your ideas. Even so, I always tried to write, read a book, go for a walk, exercise, to keep my inner self and not get depressed, because deep down I felt that I had betrayed myself, and suddenly everything vanished, that ideal to which I bet my whole being collapsed.

I saw myself alone, I felt devalued.
I had to work my pain to get to my starting point, myself. My meeting with me was like finding a treasure that I had buried and that I had forgotten. To recognize myself again, to feel myself, to recover my dreams and fulfill my goals that were stuck in obstacles in time, because there was always priority for something more important than me.

I had to feel so alone and feel loneliness to the fullest, so much silence scared me, but I learned to listen to myself in the silence, to see myself in the haze of my doubts and insecurities, I realized that I liked myself, that I had a good time with me, I realized that I am cool. I was thinking about how much I would like to have a friend like me, that we have good time (good) and I said to myself: *"myself, you can be your best friend, if someone appears, that's good and if not, that's okay too, have a great time* ", and I learned to be my best friend, my best ally, I like to be with me and be me.

Life gave me a new opportunity to fulfill all my wishes, to be free. This freedom is wonderful, and I have open arms to embrace whatever comes. God has given me the opportunity to start over, but now with the knowledge of who I am and what I want for myself.

YOUR MY GREAT TEACHER

Years ago, I spoke with a lady who specializes in holistic healing and she told me that I was going to have a marital breakdown. I did not accept it, but life put everything in its place and this marriage ended. I remember she told me that in life everything has its times.

There are marriages that are not for life. Everything that has a beginning also has an end. I had already learned what he had to learn, laugh and cry.

There are times to laugh and times to cry; So, my recommendation when it is your turn to laugh is that you laugh until you are satisfied and fill your soul with happiness, for when it is your turn to cry you can bear so much pain.

And I was amazed, I said: *¿What? ¿An act of love?* and she said: *"Yes, because in the universe there are neither good nor bad, there are only teachers who cross your path to teach you something."* It reminds me of the phrase "*I am neither judge nor executioner of anybody.*" (no soy Juez ni Verdugo) There are mysteries in life that you cannot understand or explain, and this is one of them.

I THANK YOU MY GREAT MASTER

"Today, I thank you, my best teacher, because you taught me to be strong, and you don't know how strong you are until you see yourself fighting for your life".

I let you go because you were no longer for me, and I returned to me, to be who I am, I like myself, I feel alive, happy, I feel such big and beautiful wings, that I can fly without any fear, I fly with all freedom and I enjoy the air that passes by my side when I am planning in the heights of a blue sky that has no limits, because I have myself. "I thank you for being my best teacher. "

BIOGRAPHY

María de la Luz Gutiérrez, was born in Mexico City and immigrated to the United States 30 years ago, resides in the city of Los Angeles, California. She is the mother of three children. She studied accounting, hypnotherapy, and is a businesswoman as well as a writer.

In the wake of chronic depression more than twenty years ago, she made the decision to study holistic healing techniques and become a certified Hypnotherapist. To later create the BLENDESSENCE line of oils for the beauty of the skin, an Elixir of Youth.

After 30 years of marriage, she faces the emotional blow of divorce,
which, in her own words said, "emotionally unbalanced me until I hit rock bottom and lost my identity." This inspired her to write her experience to support people who are going through a divorce process, have already been through it, or are stuck in indecision.

María de la Luz is also the Director of Public Relations for Chicas Mom, Inc. a non-profit organization dedicated to empowering the Hispanic community in the United States.

María's objective is to create an awakening of conscience, especially in women, so that they recognize their potential, and create their emotional and economic independence.

You can contact for a personal consultation and follow social networks for special events or questions:

elpoderdesanacionestaenti@gmail.com
BalanceEmocional1@gmail.com
Loslibroscambianvidas@gmail.com

Balancemocional_Hipnoterapia
Loslibroscambianvidas
Blend_Essence
BlendEssence
Los libros cambian vidas
Balance Emocional a través de Hipnoterapia

DISCLAIMER

All characters and events in this book
even those based on real people —are entirely fictional.

The information in this book is not intended as a substitute for professional legal advice in the process of a legal divorce.

The information in this book is not a substitute for professional psychological and / or medical care or support.

The author and publisher disclaim any liability in connection with the use of this information.

BIBLIOGRAFIA DE REFERENCIA

Rodolfo Gallo Pérez
Psicólogo Clínico, Psicoterapeuta cognitivo.

Mi mejor versión. YouTube channel Host by
Martha Debayle, invitados
Mario Guerra Psicoterapeuta y
Tere Diaz Psicoterapeuta familiar con
especialidad en terapia de pareja.

Beliefers. YouTube Chanel
Es un espacio donde encontraras mensajes
positivos, inspiradores frases para la vida.

Paulo Coelho, book
The Alchemist

You can't afford the luxury of a negative
though by Peter McWilliams

Are you getting enlightened or losing your
mind by Dennis Gersten, M.D.

Hablan las paredes (TRED)YouTube

Elizabeth Gilbert´s memoir Eat, Pray, Love
chronicles the journey of self-discovery

Parejas y vidas pasadas. Invitada: Maribel Pereira especialista en terapia de respuesta espiritual.

Pastor Freddy DeAnda
No luches por algo que Dios quiere que sueltes.

José Luis Rueda (CIRCA) ¿Qué está pasando con las parejas y matrimonios a nivel mundial?

YouTube Chanel
Gerardo Amaro
La historia oculta de la energía sexual.

Aurelio Mejía Hipnosis Clínica
Regresión de vidas pasadas.

Matías De Stefano
Transformación a nivel planetario.

Lucia Martine
La mujer exitosa en AA.

¿Sabes que esconde una relación Íntima?
Energías y sus consecuencias
Chanel Poder del ser. YouTube Chanel

Dios te habla escúchalo
Rhema Paraguay.

Kobe Bryant
Mamba Mentality
The Leap tv

The mind of Kobe Bryant
Piotrekzprod

Adicto a una mujer
Andrés Coate AA

Marie Curie
Documentary
Mr. Sizemik

Daniel Cerezo ¿Qué es la pobreza? El desafío de la vida en primera persona. TEDx El dorado.

Index

Made in the USA
Columbia, SC
26 November 2021